GODS INVISIBLE HAND UPON AN UNLIKELY SOLDIER

GODS INVISIBLE HAND UPON AN UNLIKELY SOLDIER

By Major General (Ret)

Richard A. Scholtes

God's Invisible Hand Upon An Unlikely Soldier

Scripture are taken from the New American Standard Bible ®, Copyright © 1960, 1962, 1963, 1968, 1971, 1972, 1973, 1975, 1977, 1995 by The Lockman Foundation. Used by permission unless otherwise marked. All rights reserved.

Cover design by Alexys Vaulkenroth of *The Camel's Brush*
Interior design by Fiverr, Aalisha
Editors: Pamela M. Scholtes, author Alexys V. Wolf

The opinions expressed by the author are those of MG (Ret) Richard A. Scholtes.

Kindle Direct Publishing

Published in the United States of America

ISBN: 9781088535561

1. Military / Autobiography / Biography

TABLE OF CONTENTS

PREFACE

This book covers many highlights of my life for the past 85 years. It all began in 1934 when I was born to a wonderful family of my mom (Josephine), my dad (Nicholas), and my brother (Ray) who was three years my senior. We were a Catholic family that attended church weekly. Ray and I attended Catholic schools and we served as altar boys. Sounds like a good Christian family, but now, looking back so many years, I recall that one significant Christian item was missing. I never saw a Bible in our home. We never discussed anything from the Bible. Sunday Catholic mass included two readings and the gospel from the Bible, but there was seldom, if ever, teaching about the readings or the gospel. We knew a few memorized prayers and, within the writings of this book, you will find numerous times when I prayed those prayers so hard each time a major life-changing event was taking place.

The significance of the fact that we did not have or ever discuss the content of the Bible did not surface until very late in my life. I had always looked at the Bible as a group of writings by many different authors at many different times. I never looked upon it as the true Word of God. It was not until after the turn of the century in the years 2008 to 2013 that someone very special gave me my first personalized Bible and a minister at a new church enlightened me that the Bible was in fact the infallible Word of God. The writings were by different men at different times, but regardless, they were guided solely by God as they wrote what were the Words of God. It is those words that helped me write this book. It is a synopsis of a long life that was guided by God where major events that impacted my life were made and driven by my God.

INTRODUCTION

In our lifetime, we can all expect to face many decisions and to live through many events which will impact the remainder of our time here on Earth. Think of how many critical decisions concerning your work and career you have already made. Think of so many unplanned or unprogrammed events which impacted you and yours. Can't remember all of them? How about back in your childhood days, your schooling days, right up to your now days. You may recall many or just a few, but can you remember instances where a decision or crucial event was not of your doing? You probably remember decisions on a significant job opportunity that headed you in the right direction. But how about when, out of the blue, without any thought or effort on your part, a new and improved series of decisions or events provided an even better opportunity with better results. Any decisions ring a bell?

Over the next few chapters, I will discuss some paramount decisions and milestones in my life. They had tremendous impact on the direction and quality of my life, but many of these decisions and events were not of my making. At first, I thought these happenings just occurred without thought or effort. I now realize that I was not the decision maker. These non-decisions seemed to have a much greater impact on my life than most of my own decisions that I thought were great. Then who guided the decision-making? As I relate the full impact of some of these decisions, it will become apparent that they were managed from outside my capacity. Read on and you too might find that some decisions and events that impacted your life came from the greatest Friend anyone could ever have – our heavenly Father.

CHAPTER I

EARLY YEARS

Many years ago, in the city of Joliet in the state of Illinois, I became a member of a super family with my mom Josephine, my dad Nicholas, and my brother Raymond (Ray). Dad was born in the country of Luxembourg to a stone-cutting father and he came to the States at a very early age. As an adult, dad was also a stone-cutter who could carve a beautiful statue from a large block of stone. Mom was an excellent mother who worked many hard jobs in the local brickyard and coke factory. The family made 4 moves in my childhood and, to me and Ray, the best move was to the country where he could master his skill of fishing while I tried to master my skill of hunting rabbits, squirrels, and pheasant. This was an early indication of my appreciation for weapons. My folks had given me a .22/410 over and under for my 10th birthday and, if you ever tried shooting a running wild rabbit with a gun with a small shot pattern like a 410, you know the difficulty. I was never as good as I wanted to be, but Ray and I helped to provide many supper meals of fish or game. As I look back to those days so long ago, there were many instances where my Lord interceded on my behalf when I was completely unaware that He was even present. There was one early happening where His presence was truly evident.

The incident took place at about the age of six. It could have killed me or, at the very least, scarred me for life. My brother and I were playing pirate in the house. To better play the role, I had a sash around my waist with one of Mom's butcher knives stuck inside. I was looking for my hidden brother and was holding the knife in my hand. When Ray ran from one room to another, I ran after him. The small rug in front of the couch caught my foot and I fell forward. My hand with the knife hit the floor with the blade point up and my face heading directly at the knife point! Somehow, my entire body stopped in midair for a split second with the knife point inches away. My body rolled away from the knife and I fell harmlessly to the floor. To this day, I remember every detail of that split second. I had made the stupid decision to take the knife from the drawer, a really dumb choice to have the knife in my hand, and then the stupidest of decisions to run with the knife. God, and only God, could have done what He did. I dread the thought if God had not taken pity on a young boy's lousy decision making.

Some years later, I worked long and hard at trying to convince my mother that I should transfer from the Catholic school to a public school. Most of my friends attended Farragut Junior High School which, in those days, was 7th and 8th grade. There was also the cost of the Catholic school versus the public school, so I tried that for leverage to sell the idea. My rationale was that, if I could convince mom for the transfer to a public grade school, I could later work on her to go to the public high school where they offered trade industrial courses to include wood working. My plan was to be a carpenter, so all of this made sense at the time. Fortunately for me, my God had different plans.

My mother finally agreed to the transfer to Farragut Junior High School where I completed the 7th and 8th grades and was anxious to enter. Mom and I had discussed my attending the public high school so that I could take woodworking. When Mom said, "Yes," I took the first opportunity to go to the administrative offices and sign up for

Photo #1: Mom, Dad, Grandma, Ray and me 1940

woodworking. The high school was very large with over a thousand students in each grade. Finding one's way around the school was quite a struggle but, in the process, I noted something strange. Several of my classmates were wearing white shirts and ties to class on certain days of the week. Curiosity got the best of me, so I found a friend who was wearing the shirt and tie and I asked him what the deal was. He informed me that he was in the ROTC (Reserve Officer Training Corps), and that, as freshman, they had to wear the shirt and tie for drill periods each week. But, as sophomores, juniors, and seniors, they would be issued regular Army uniforms.

I do not know why, but that sparked some interest. Though I always planned on carpentry as my goal for the future, now something was pulling me toward the ROTC. Some might argue that the pull toward ROTC was from the family, but I know that was not possible because my father and his nine brothers and sisters had very little trust or faith in the military because of what the German Army did to their homeland of Luxembourg. Then there was also the issue of whether the school administration would allow a major change in curriculum. I decided to at least talk to the people in charge of the ROTC. I found their offices and, with some trepidation, I entered. There were two men in uniforms and I asked them about the ROTC program and if they thought there was a chance the school would allow a change of schedule. They gave me brochures to read about ROTC and said they would talk to the administration if I elected to add ROTC to my schedule.

Several days passed as I mulled things over. Finally, I worked up the gumption to talk to the administration. The lady at the office was very helpful and, after some finagling, she informed me she could change my schedule to allow woodworking and ROTC; however, some of my other courses would have to be dropped which didn't bother me at all. I was very excited with the news and gave the go ahead without truly appreciating the possible ramifications like, "What will Mom and Dad say," or "What about those courses that were being dropped?" Once again, the good Lord had interceded on my behalf without me ever appreciating the fact. My entry into the ROTC program would have a most significant impact on the remainder of my life.

My four years in the ROTC program provided many opportunities to do some things I never anticipated. We marched in parades for Veterans Day, the 4th of July, Flag Day, and many others. Each year we sponsored a formal military ball for the entire senior class. This required extensive decorations of the school gymnasium and installation of additional lighting. Selecting the right band for this affair was critical. Remember, this was in the early 50's and there was a wide assortment of music, so the band selection committee was careful not to select from the far ends of the music spectrum. Another ROTC activity that I personally enjoyed and took an active part was our school rifle team. This offered me an opportunity to travel to numerous different schools in Northern Illinois for competitive shooting matches. We also had a six-point practice range in the school right next to the ROTC offices. In addition to the learning associated with the activities already mentioned was the learning of something very important. That was the value and necessity for rigid discipline in a military force.

Something that would normally be very insignificant occurred my sophomore year. One of the ROTC noncommissioned officers was talking to several of us cadets and mentioned some work he was doing with the local unit of the Illinois National Guard. This piqued my interest, and, after several rounds of questions, I learned that the local unit of the Guard was a rifle company and they were looking for additional volunteers. I knew from answers to my earlier questions that the age requirement for joining was 18. I failed to meet it by almost three years and I could think of only one alternative to overcome this problem. It would require some incorrect data concerning my date of birth being inserted on the application to be signed by my parents. I put the National Guard decision on a back burner, but continued thought of giving it a try.

Photo #2-: Junior ROTC 1050

CHAPTER 2

DUTY WITH THE ILLINOIS NATIONAL GUARD

At the halfway point of our junior year in 1950, the thought of joining the National Guard became a priority consideration. Looking back, I see several times in my early years where the good Lord pointed me in a direction I had not anticipated. Joining ROTC was a first step and joining the National Guard was the second step. So, off I went figuring "nothing ventured, nothing gained." I proceeded to the National Guard office where I was given additional information, some brochures, and forms to be completed by my parents. I read the brochures and completed the forms as required with one major exception. I entered a date of birth with a minor error (a lie) showing I was 18 years old. My mother never read the application before signing it; therefore, immediately after it was signed, I delivered the papers to the unit. A week or so later, I went through a swearing in ceremony and became an official member of Company G, 129th Infantry Regiment, 4th Infantry Division, of the Illinois National Guard.

My first two years with the Guard were a true learning experience. I thought I knew some things about the military, but rapidly learned

I was a true beginner. Our unit required everyone to attend a two-hour training period every week. At these sessions, we learned everything from our individual weapons to the larger crew served weapons that required three or more soldiers to carry and operate the weapon. Time was also spent on small unit tactics where we learned the movement techniques and security requirements. The highlight each year was summer encampment where our units traveled from Illinois to Camp McCoy, Wisconsin, or Camp Ripley, Minnesota for training and military exercises. I was fortunate to receive promotions to corporal and later to sergeant my first year with the unit. I was also very fortunate that there were several older members of the unit that had served in WWII. These old-timers had lived through several battles and helped us new guys a great deal. In 1950, I was selected to attend a three week leadership school in Fort Knox, Kentucky. That brief course of instruction was one more step in the direction of a military career.

In 1951, our unit received a terrific jolt when we were notified that our National Guard Division was being federalized for duty in Korea. You will recall that the United States, as part of the United Nations, was at war with North Korea. This all occurred at the same time I was scheduled to graduate high school. At least I thought I was graduating only to learn that my dedication to woodworking and the National Guard impacted the time I devoted to other subjects. I had failed one subject. To graduate, I needed to attend summer school, but my dilemma was summer school or deployment with the unit to Camp Cooke, California. Once again, the good Lord came to my rescue with some key decisions. I was informed that instead of deploying with the unit to Camp Cooke, I would be attending several special training programs at the Infantry School, Fort Benning, Georgia, and then join the unit in California. These programs had a starting date much later than our initial deployment would have required. It permitted my attendance at a condensed summer school so that I could receive my High school diploma.

When summer school was completed, I received my diploma and prepared for and made the trip to Fort Benning, Georgia. The course of instruction was entitled, "Light and Heavy Weapons Leadership Course." It was outstanding preparation for what I envisioned would be needed when my unit arrived in Korea. The course was several weeks long and my mom and dad drove down one weekend. I showed them around Fort Benning, we took in a movie, and just spent time relaxing. Following graduation, I returned to Illinois for a few days and then had to fly from Chicago to California to join my unit. Camp Cooke was an old Army post used for armored forces training and preparing for deployment to Europe during WWII. It consists of 90,000 acres with 35 miles of coastline on the Pacific Ocean. Camp Cooke provided everything the division needed for training except for mountains such as we would find in Korea. The division commander had obviously considered the need for some mountain training because he announced that we were to wrap up our preparations with a four-week exercise in the mountains of Hunter Ligget in the California high country.

Prior to departing for our final training exercise at Hunter Ligget, we were given two days rest and recuperation at Camp Cooke. During this break, some friends and I decided to take in a movie, "Francis Goes to West Point." It was about a talking mule named Francis at the Military Academy at West Point in New York. Little did I imagine the impact of that movie on my future. Our Lord was apparently clearing a path for me that I never could have imagined. As I left the theater, I was stopped by a Captain Rossi who said he was our Battalion Adjutant. He asked if I had ever considered going to West Point. My answer was an immediate, "NO SIR." I knew with my high school record almost any thought of college was out of the question. He did not accept the answer and informed me he had received materiel from the Army concerning selection of a small number of National Guard soldiers to attend the United States Military Academy (USMA) Preparatory school. He told me to come to his office after the evening meal so he could show me the documents he had received. He indicated he had to have the required forms mailed to Department of the Army in just three days. I hurried with my meal and returned to his office to learn that he had not received the printed forms that were required for the application. He began to draw up the forms from photos in the Army Regulations book. I do not know how he did it, but he worked long and hard and, when the forms were completed, I signed them and returned to my barracks where I packed and prepared to depart for our final exercise. I never gave the forms about West Point much thought because the war in Korea was my primary concern.

The Hunter Ligget exercise was a true learning experience for so many of us who knew little or nothing about movement in mountainous terrain. We learned fast that the impact of walking on the slope of the mountains was very tough on the feet. We also learned that socks, wet from rain and perspiration, would also have a deleterious effect on the feet. Blisters were everywhere and the medics did their best to keep up with the problem feet. Vehicle drivers also learned the hazards of steep slope driving. Try as they may, even in four-wheel drive, movement straight up the slopes was almost impossible. Driving across the slope was a good solution for medium angles of slope but, when they changed to steep, it was a different story. The first several days we were simulating offensive operations which required rapid movement from mountain to mountain. The squad learned quickly that our machine guns and other equipment became a heavy burden on those hills. When we reverted to defensive operations, there was much less movement and it was a welcome relief.

As we approached the final rehearsal of tactical exercises, I received another jolt that showed me, once again, our good Lord had things under His control. A messenger arrived on the hilltop where my unit was deployed and informed me that I had to go back to the company command post some distance from my location. Apparently, a message had arrived at the command post and the commander wanted me to read it. I could not imagine why they wanted me, a

Photo #3: MG Hartness wishing me well 1952

squad leader and not much more. I trekked the long route back to the company headquarters location. The company commander informed me that I was to return to Camp Cooke as soon as possible because of something to do with West Point. God, in His wonderful way, was directing everything on my behalf.

I finally caught a ride on a supply truck that was returning to Camp Cooke and, during that long trip, I had a lot of time to try and determine precisely what was going on. Upon arrival, I immediately went to the post headquarters because the entire division was still at Hunter Ligget. There the duty officer informed me of a message from Department of the Army. The message was difficult for a young sergeant to comprehend because I had never seen anything like it. The duty officer read it and told me it read that I was reassigned from the 44th National Guard Division and was to report to the United States Military Academy Preparatory School located at Stewart AFB in Newburg, New York on a specified date in the future. I was more than speechless and found it hard to believe what I was hearing. I had never heard of a preparatory school and wondered what it did. I could not imagine after my high school years that anyone would consider me qualified to go to any college, much less the Military Academy at West Point. The duty officer took me to another office and introduced me to a warrant officer who would handle my paperwork. The warrant officer hit me immediately with a question about how my age in the National Guard paperwork failed to match my age from official birth records. He explained that my enlistment in the National Guard was under fraudulent conditions and he wanted clarification. I told him the truth about how I had fibbed (lied) about my age. He then informed me that, since I was now of proper age, he would correct all the records before he forwarded them to DA and the USMA Preparatory School. He also said he was preparing the flight schedule to New York and noted I would change planes in Chicago. I asked if I could take a few days leave in Illinois. He checked my leave status and agreed to seven days. This would give me

Photo #4: USMA Prep School 1952

a chance to tell my folks firsthand what was happening. That is, of course, *if* I could get my mind around everything that was happening. Once again, major decisions were being made that were void of any input from me, but I look back and know my heavenly Father was intimately involved in all these decisions.

CHAPTER 3

FROM WAR TO WEST POINT

Departing Camp Cooke, going through the Los Angeles Airport, changing planes in Chicago, and finally arriving in New York was a unique experience for someone who had never been very far from his hometown. You may recall that there were no jet airliners at that time, so the long trip in a prop-driven aircraft allowed me time to try and collect my thoughts. On arrival in New York, I went directly to the USO information booth at the terminal and was given information as to how to get to Stewart AFB. The trip entailed taking a cab to Grand Central Station in downtown New York, then taking the train to a stop across the Hudson from Newburg, New York, then a trek across the bridge into Newburg, and finally a taxi to the Air Force base. All sounded very easy but, when you are dragging two large suitcases without wheels while wearing a uniform that you do not want to become a wrinkled mess, it was a little difficult. Back in the 1950's, soldiers were not allowed to ever travel in their fatigue uniforms as they are today. We wore the uniform with the waist length Ike jacket named for General Eisenhower. It included a dress shirt and tie. Getting to the train terminal was easy, but walking to the proper train number at the largest train station I had ever seen was much harder. I finally made it and, after stowing the suitcases, I was on my way. I found a seat next to an elderly gentleman. He asked me where I was going. I told him about the prep school and he told me to look out the window on the Hudson side of the train. In a short time, we passed directly across from the academy at West Point. It was a beautiful view of the academy. The buildings, the grounds, and (what I later learned was the chapel) were impressive sights.

Next came the stop across from Newburgh, New York. From what I had been told by the people at the USO, I figured the bridge to Newburgh would be a short stroll. No, this bridge across the Hudson river looked more like a mile. The suitcases and I made the trek to Newburgh only to learn later that I could have phoned for a taxi at the offloading site. I finally made it and, upon arriving at Stewart AFB, I was directed to the preparatory school headquarters. From there, I was assigned to a bunk and a wall locker in one of two student barracks. For the next several hours, I had an opportunity to meet soldiers, sailors, airmen, and marines that were my classmates attempting to undergo academic training to prepare us all for possible entry into the military academy. Over the next week, I learned how my decision to drop so many classes in high school was going to make life more stressful. We were informed that the first step in the process was to take an exam designed to give the instructors an idea as to where each candidate stood academically. I recall that I did not just take the exam. No, I struggled to even get through it. There were so many questions that I had no idea as to what it all meant. As a result, I had a special meeting with the colonel, the dean of the school. He informed me that I had not only failed the exam, but I had received the lowest number of correct answers in the history of the exam! He told me he saw very little hope for me to pass the West Point entrance exam. However, he said they would do everything to give me a chance by giving me additional training each night. I am convinced that their decision was not the norm for this school, but my God played the critical role in giving me a chance.

Over the next several months, I spent what seemed like every waking hour on something to do with math, algebra, calculus, science, geometry, trigonometry, and engineering. The instructors, who were all military officers, were great and went out of their way to help me. Even with a great deal of assistance, I was very concerned about the probability of success, but looking in the rear-view mirror was of no use because the time had come. As we sat at small tables, we were handed the packet – the entrance examination for the United States Military Academy. I do not recall how many questions were included, but the sheer volume of the packet caused concern. We all concentrated solely on the exam for the next several hours. As each candidate completed their exam, they gave it to the instructor and departed the room.

As we left the exam room, the immediate question by those already out there was, "How do you think you did?" and the answer from most was, "Man, I don't know. That was one tough exam!" Then the waiting period began as the exams were graded. It was a rough several days and, finally, we were given the exam results. I was shocked, amazed, and thrilled that all the sweat and sleepless nights were well worth it. I had passed! The immediate reaction by many was to give yourself a solid pat on the back for a job well done. But, was it solely my effort that gave me the passing grade? I know that any credit that was due goes exclusively to my heavenly Father.

What I failed to understand, at that time, was that these exams were being taken nationwide and there were many in the competitive grouping like the National Guard. When the results were reviewed on a nationwide basis, I received a serious punch in the gut. I was informed that I was fully qualified but, due to the limited number of spaces available for National Guard competitive appointments, there was no vacancy. I do not know the exact number of candidates that could be selected from the National Guard, but the number that passed the exam and the physical tests exceeded the number of spaces available. I did not make the cut line.

Several classmates also missed the cut line, so we decided to drive to Washington to determine if we could possibly receive a Senatorial or House of Representatives appointment. Off we drove in two candidates' cars from New York to Washington, D.C. On arrival, we stopped at the Pentagon and informed the academy selection personnel what we were doing. Then we split up and proceeded to the halls of the Senate Office Building. We spent hours walking the halls and talking to senators or their secretaries. At the hour we specified, we all gathered for the trip back to the Pentagon and then to New York. Much to my disappointment, I was unable to get an appointment from the congressmen. Some of the guys were able to secure 3rd or 4th alternate appointments, but the chance of a principal or 1st or 2nd alternate not meeting all standards would be rare. While checking in at the Pentagon, those that had received new alternate appointments had to fill out additional forms. As we were about to leave, one of the officers asked me to come to his office. There he informed me that one of the National Guard men had failed either the exam or the physical test, so I was next in line to fill the National Guard appointments. Some might say I was just lucky, but I will always believe that my Lord played the primary role in my being eligible to fill the final Guard appointment.

In June 1953, the Military Academy Class of 1957 was sworn in at Trophy Point at West Point. Thanks to my heavenly Father for some very heavy lifting, I became a member of that class. That very day, all "New Cadets" learned why they have named the first several months at the academy "Beast Barracks." Every waking moment of every day of these three months, the new cadets were under eyes of the First Classman assigned to the "Beast Detail." Having ROTC and the National Guard experiences made this period of indoctrination a little easier. The Beast Detail had the task of converting the new cadet class into West Point cadets. Every waking moment, you were under the scrutiny of members of the Beast Detail. They used the name "dumb smack" and others as the titles for all new cadets. Those who have lived through this indoctrination will attest to the unique nature of this conversion. It is the toughness of this program and a strict academic requirement that makes the academy and its graduates what it really is!

My Plebe (freshman) year was not the finest year of my life. Academics were tough and, in several cases, required tutoring by our more intelligent classmates. This tutoring was accomplished in what the cadets refer to as the "sinks." In fact, it is where the showers are in the basement of the building. Those cadets having academic problems meet as groups depending on the subject. Two or three classmates will answer questions and give instruction where necessary. In December, we had a great break from academics for two weeks. It was Plebe Christmas when all the upper classmen took leave and the Plebe class oversaw everything. There was still a great emphasis on discipline because we had to remember the tactical officers were ever present. My fiancée, JoAnn, flew up and spent a few days. As a result, we had to remember what the upper classmen had said about PDA (public display of affection). It was never allowed and would result in a slug, which meant at least eight hours walking the area at attention with your rifle. PDA was defined as holding hands, kissing, hugging, or arm around the waist or shoulders.

As we approached the end of this first year, I had an accident in gym class. I fell during a rope climb and was knocked unconscious. The medical staff thought it serious enough to commit me to the hospital. I was informed that I was awake upon arrival in the hospital, but I have no recollection of those three days. The medical staff told me I seemed confused and had difficulty accepting where I was. They thought it was a form of amnesia. Thankfully, I snapped out of it after three days, but then faced the likelihood of termination from the academy for medical reasons. Here again, when I went before a medical board, my Lord was at my side because I handled the numerous questions with no difficulty and with terminology I could not have mustered on my own. The result was approval of my

Photo #5: Plebe year cadet photo 1953

remaining as a cadet, but my records would be sent to the Army and would eliminate me from seeking a pilot rating in the future.

Yearling (sophomore) year was like Plebe year as far as academics were concerned. I did not have to rely as heavily on help from others, but it was more difficult than I preferred. I mention the problems with academics because that was where I was most concerned. Of lesser concern, but still very significant, was the military side of the academy that also demanded time and effort. There were parades on the large plain where hundreds of spectators gathered each week. In the winter, parades were called "Band Box Reviews" and were conducted in the cadet barracks area. All Saturday parades were conducted after the entire corps underwent the infamous "SAMI," (Saturday morning inspection) where every cadet's room was inspected by the tactical officer. The tiniest speck of dust could gain you considerable demerits.

If that was not enough, the room inspection was followed by an in-ranks inspection. I recall one such inspection in full dress uniforms. As the officer moved to a position in front of a cadet, the cadet brought his rifle to what is called the "Port Arms" position where he opens the bolt and waits. The inspector would take the rifle and examine every part of the weapon as well as the cadet's uniform. I thought I was doing well with the inspection until the officer said, "Mister Scholtes, you have dust on your dress coat buttons." Can you imagine something as insignificant as a little dust on a button of my uniform? As soon as we were released and I went to my room, I checked every button on the full-dress coat and, sure enough, there was dust on several of the buttons. That never happened again, but it meant four demerits. After 12 to 14 demerits per month, the cadet must walk the area at attention for an hour with his rifle for each demerit over that number. I was fortunate because that dust on a button did not put me over the limit. I also learned it only takes a couple seconds to wipe all the buttons on a full-dress uniform.

Earlier in the Yearling year, I had selected Spanish as my foreign language. Several told me it would be the easiest. As we prepared

Photo #6: Howie and me 1955

for the end of year, I felt comfortable with the WGR's (written general reviews), which were like the final exams for most college courses. Then as I approached the Spanish classroom for the WGR, the Mexican officer who was our instructor stopped me and said something like, "Cadet Scholtes, if you do not score better than 82 on this WGR, I am afraid you will be found for academic deficiency." My mind went racing and I am sure my classmates were wondering why I was sweating so profusely. For those of you who do not understand the West Point lingo, he was telling me I would be kicked out of the academy if I did not score above this number. I think I was the last cadet to leave that exam room and, I must admit, I said so many prayers during that exam I cannot count them. I should clarify that, with my Catholic upbringing I never appreciated that prayer was more than memorized phrases but was in fact talking to God. I knew the "Our Father" the "Hail Mary," and the "Act of Contrition" verbatim and in a crisis, I would repeat them hundreds of times. In this case, my heavenly Father, being omniscient, understood my situation and He came through.

Next came Cow (junior) year with a warning from everyone that this would be the toughest academic year of all. I had just completed two of the most difficult academic years of my life and did not appreciate this warning. However, before we could wrestle with the academic year, we had to go on what is referred to as "the Cow Trip." This trip took the class to every military post that was identified as the home of a branch of the Army: Fort Benning for the infantry, Fort Knox for the armor, Fort Sill for the artillery, etc. etc. This trip could be looked upon as the branch's efforts to show their best side so that those cadets could select their branch upon graduation. The end of Cow year brought more WGR's and more studying and sweat. Once again, my God had to be watching over me because I made it through without significant problems.

Now, onto my Firsty (senior) year and many major events leading up to graduation. I had been given the title of Company Commander

Photo #7: Mom and Dad graduation day 1957

of Company F of the first regiment. As with every year, there was the Army versus Navy football game, which we won. The entire corps of cadets would perform a march prior to the start of the game. Marching while wearing a full-length overcoat that feels like it weighs several hundred pounds is a difficult task. One of the more exciting events was the auto show. Dealers from the general area all converged to sell their cars to the graduating class. I went with the 1957 turquoise Chevy, 2-door sedan with stick shift. Then we had to wait until, finally, the cars were delivered. They were unloaded in a parking lot across from the Thayer Hotel at the main entrance to the academy. We could not drive them on the post, so we had to walk the half mile to the cars just to start them and do nothing more than look at them. I have not mentioned academics for Firsty year because I was confident that, if I made it this far, I would study my tail off to be certain to get that diploma.

The four years were about to end but, once again, as we approached graduation, there came the extremely important decisions associated with the selection of our branch of service and of our first duty station. Both selections were based on class standing which, in turn, were determined by individual academic performance over the four years. This, as you probably guessed, caused me considerable concern. I wanted the Infantry Branch. It was not the most popular to the remainder of the class, so did not concern myself too much with that. I wanted my duty station to be with the 82nd Airborne Division at Fort Bragg, North Carolina. On that decision, I leaned heavily on the good Lord. I know my Lord heard my prayers because both the branch and assignment came through for me.

CHAPTER 4

FROM WEST POINT TO THE 82ND AIRBORNE DIVISION

Following graduation, we had a month's leave before reporting to Fort Benning, Georgia. During the leave, I married JoAnn and together we proceeded to Fort Benning. I had to complete the Basic Infantry Officer Course (BIOC), which was 15 weeks, Airborne School to attain jump wings which was 3 weeks, and Ranger School, which was 7 weeks. The BIOC and airborne courses went very well with no competitive nature; however, Ranger School was the most difficult and demanding. It consisted of numerous patrols at Fort Benning, in the mountains near Dahlonega, Georgia, and in the Florida swamps near Eglin AFB, Florida. The term "patrol" describes a small group of soldiers who are given a mission to move into enemy territory and perform a specific task. The task might be to observe a special enemy activity and report back all that was observed, or the task might be to move to a bridge and blow it so the enemy could not use it.

With each patrol, there was a lane grader, an officer who graded the performance of the patrol leaders. For each patrol, an initial leader was selected and he would be replaced with a new leader somewhere during the patrol. Then, one or two more patrol leaders would be inserted depending on the length of the patrol. Some patrols covered many miles of movement and lasted several days. Each new patrol leader had to know precisely where the patrol was when he was given command and must inform every member of the patrol any new tasks or assignments they might have to perform at the objective. Unfortunately, no one knew who would be selected or when they would take over the patrol. Once again, I know my heavenly Father was watching over me because, when we had completed all patrols and were back at Fort Benning for graduation, I was selected as the honor graduate and given the honor graduate guide-on.

Subsequently, JoAnn and I moved to Fort Bragg, North Carolina for assignment to the 82nd Airborne Division. On arriving at Fort Bragg, I was initially assigned as a platoon leader of a rifle platoon of about 40 men. After several months, I was moved to the position as executive officer to the company commander. As second in command of the unit, I was directly involved with all personnel matters and training. I still maintained personal events as high priority and a very high priority was the birth of our son, Richard (Rick) in May 1958. Having never been associated with babies before, Rick was a true learning experience. I will always remember he would slip his feet into my loafers, put on my hat, and march around the room. He was a happy little fellow. Little did I imagine that Rick would later serve as an enlisted man, a warrant officer pilot, and an officer pilot. He flew Apache gunships in the first war with Iraq. He also ended up as a special operations pilot. While balancing his military activities, Rick met and married Sara, and they have three super children. I had to leave the family for the first major training event for the Battle Group. This was a deployment to Alaska for a major exercise lasting several weeks with the Alaskan Infantry Regiment. The second major training event was an exercise in the city of Danville, Virginia, wherein the Battle Group did an airborne assault to recapture the city from an enemy force.

Movement to Alaska was by Air Force C-124 aircraft and, while in route, my plane had engine problems and had to land in North Dakota. The C-124 was prop-driven and was the biggest airplane in the Air Force inventory in those days. The air base we landed on was in a highly restricted area and we were told not to look around or take any photos while on the ground. It was a nuclear missile site. The plane was repaired in a few hours and we were on our way to Alaska. We arrived and immediately opened a staging area to commence the exercises. We saw temperatures as low as -64 degrees while getting ready. In the middle of the exercise, my commander came to me and told me of a new mission. I was to take 40 men from our unit and prepare for an airborne assault mission. After identifying the 40 men to participate, we learned we were going to parachute into the enemy rear area, assemble, and move to positions to cut the enemy's main supply route. As we prepared, I went often to the good Lord to seek any advice or counsel concerning the welfare of the men. For all parachute jumps from Air Force aircraft, the rear of the aircraft is under control of an Air Force loadmaster, normally a senior sergeant. I was serving as the jumpmaster and I had to closely coordinate everything with the loadmaster.

In Alaska, the pilot will inform the loadmaster when the plane is 10 minutes from the drop zone. The loadmaster will then open both jump doors and the jumpmaster will lean out of the aircraft so he can observe the drop zone. Just as I was about to lean out, I felt a tug on my equipment. The loadmaster had grabbed me and was yelling to not lean out. He then had to shout over the roar of the engines that, in the Alaskan winter, you never lean out and look forward. At the speed we were traveling, well over 120 miles per hour, in a temperature of -30 degrees, my eyes would have frozen instantly, and my face would have suffered frostbite. I did not stick my head out but trusted the pilots when they turned on the green light, the signal to exit the plane. Everyone exited the aircraft in good shape and then came the landing. We landed on a large lake and the snow was well over 6 feet deep.

We had to use our bear paws which were lashed to our sides to dig ourselves out. Digging out sounds like a simple thing but remember, this is Alaska and each soldier is wearing arctic clothing, his weapon, his parachute harness, and gear to carry ammunition, water, and a knife. Bear paws are like snowshoes but smaller in size. Once we dug ourselves out, we had to fix the bear paws to our boots for walking. That sounds easy but, in the 6-foot-deep snow, it meant lying on your back and working to place the bear paws in position and lash them to the boots while you slowly sank into the snow. Once everyone was prepared, we started movement to an assembly area in the trees surrounding the lake. We had also parachuted skis in bundles on sleds called "ahkios." These sleds also held our tents and space heaters.

In the assembly area, we lashed the skis to our boots and were ready to move out. After miles of cross-country skiing, we came across the enemy supply road which was cut through the snow. We set up our ambush and awaited the enemy. When trucks arrived, we ambushed them and were able to maintain control of the enemy's main route of supply until the end of the exercise. I would like to take full credit for the success of the mission, but I know the real credit goes to God who had His hand in every phase of the operation. These 40 soldiers had skied cross-country over 30 miles, often in sub-zero temperatures, and never suffered a single case of frostbite.

The exercise in Danville did not have the dangers of freezing temperature or extremely rugged terrain but, once again, God was present. The parachute jump was conducted in a little more wind than was preferred, but we did not have any serious injuries. We had vehicles going in every direction in the city along with the normal traffic, but there were no serious accidents. The people of Danville were tremendous in their support. When that many soldiers and vehicles invade a town for 24 hours and no one gets seriously hurt, we must thank Jesus our Lord.

When we returned to Fort Bragg and were settled into a normal routine, I, along with several junior officers and senior non-commissioned officers, received word that we were being reassigned to the US Southern Command with station in Panama. Apparently, the Army staff had directed that a new Ranger Battalion be formed in Panama. Married personnel were advised that dependents would not accompany them but would be permitted to join their spouses in four to six months. I took some leave so I could take the family back to Joliet to stay with JoAnn's mother and father. I drove to Charleston AFB where I was to fly from there to Panama. I also arranged for shipment of my car to Panama. I flew by military air from Charleston to Panama and arrived at the Air Force base on the Pacific side of the isthmus. I was transported across the isthmus to the Atlantic coast where I joined several others on the same orders at Fort Gulick. As I entered the Fort, I noticed it was extremely well kept with numerous brick buildings, which I later discovered were the home of the US Army Caribbean Command Language School. It was not until the next morning that I saw Fort William D. Davis, where the new Ranger battalion would be stationed. This fort was last used in World War II and was in dire need of more than a face lift. Regardless, it was our new home for the next several years and we figured a new Ranger Battalion would get this place looking great in a few weeks.

Then, as we tried to figure where to start, we received news that was not well accepted by any of us. The Army had changed its mind and, instead of a Ranger Battalion, we were to form an Infantry Battle Group. Anyone in the Army who is not airborne qualified would never appreciate what this meant to the cadre of personnel already in place. These men were all senior or master parachute jumpers with years of experience. In addition to the airborne experience, there is the pride and spirit that is present in every Ranger unit, which is rarely found in other units. There is also the loss of jump pay which is approximately $110.00 per month, and that was very important since the basic pay for a lieutenant was only $291.00 per month. Many of the senior non-commissioned officers who had 20 years of service put in their retirement papers saying they did not want to serve their final years

Photo #8: Company B Commander in Panama 1961

in a leg (non-airborne) Battle Group. I even remember praying that this could not be happening. This time, the Lord apparently did not agree with me.

At this time, the Battle Group had no filler soldiers since they had not arrived from the states. The only personnel assigned were junior officers in the grade of lieutenant and captain, and senior non-commissioned officers in the grades of sergeant first class and above. Through the efforts of this cadre, Fort William D. Davis was gradually taking on a military appearance. Thankfully, the day came when the troops began arriving by the busloads. The commander assigned me to the headquarters company of the Battle Group as the executive officer. I was also informed that we could bring our families to the Canal Zone. I arranged for housing for the family and then called JoAnn and informed her that she and Rick should fly to Charleston and then taxi to what was called Charleston Air Force base. They would then fly to Howard Air Force Base in the Canal Zone and I would pick them up for the drive across the isthmus. The trip went well for their travels as well as the move into our quarters on Fort Davis. The housing was furnished so, fortunately, we did not need our furniture shipped to the Canal Zone. The quarters had no air conditioning and, since JoAnn was pregnant now with our second child, the Panama heat was stifling. All the windows were glass louvered, so I removed enough of the glass slats on one window to install a large window air conditioner. It worked great and made it so much more comfortable. It was expensive, but well worth the cost.

Our son Thomas (Tom) was born in 1961 at the Coco Solo Naval Hospital in the Canal Zone. Later, when Tom was in high school, the Army reassigned me every year. We went from Germany to West Point, and then to Virginia, and finally to Fort Bragg in North Carolina. Our rapid reassignments caused Tom to attend four different high schools. In fact, I believe he has the wrong class ring because of 4 moves in

4 years. Here again, I never thought that Tom would also become a soldier. The real surprise came when Tom decided he was going to the Military Academy. Tom ran into a bureaucratic mess when he applied. They thought he was born in a foreign country and as a result he was not qualified to enter the academy. Convincing everyone that Coco Solo Naval Hospital was part of the Canal Zone, which was United States property, was difficult, but he won and graduated in 1983 as an armored officer. When Tom went to Airborne School, I was fortunate to be able to join him for his fifth and final jump. It's a strange feeling when you watch your son jump from an aircraft and then follow directly behind him – or did Tom follow me – regardless, it's a strange feeling. Tom was fortunate to find and marry Beth and, they have 5 amazing children.

The months passed slowly as we worked to form the Battle Group into a disciplined outfit. Then one sunny afternoon, a terrible accident happened. The 5 senior staff officers of the Battle Group, all Lieutenant Colonels or Majors, were flying to Fort Amador on the Pacific side of the isthmus when the plane carrying them crashed killing everyone. As far as I know, they were never able to ascertain what caused that fateful crash. When the bodies were retrieved, I was given the task of sorting through everything those officers had on or with them when they crashed. It was a miserable assignment, but we wanted to ensure that the families received everything which was rightfully theirs. It took the Battle Group a long time to get over this tragic loss.

When the Battle Group was filled with soldiers from the states, we began an extensive training program starting with the basics. Our primary training area was at Rio Hato about 110 miles from Fort Davis. As the units became more involved with training, I was reassigned to become the 4.2" Mortar Platoon leader. Ironically, in the past, this weapon was always assigned to the artillery trained soldiers, but now a group of infantrymen who knew little or nothing about this weapon were given the mission of being able to provide heavy mortar fire support to the entire Battle Group. I won't bore you with all the problems we encountered, but my learning curve had to do some rapid growth. Here is an example of the problems we faced the day we first fired the mortars.

When the forward observer who selects the target radioed in for fire on a burned-out vehicle on the range, the FDC (Fire Direction Center) that provides weapon setting to the gun crews informed the forward observer the target was out of range. Then an argument began. The FDC soldiers had done their homework and knew the maximum range was 4,400 yards or about 2 ½ miles. That afternoon, we had another training session for the entire outfit. I spent a great deal of time at night asking a lot of favors of my heavenly Father and He delivered. The platoon did well in support of the Battle Group annual training test.

I was promoted to captain in December 1961 and was given command of company B, 2nd Battle Group, 10th Infantry, a rifle company. Having had a chance to observe the training being conducted in the past, I was concerned that we were not placing enough emphasis in the jungle training of our units. The field training of all units was accomplished at the Rio Hato training area and it had no jungle environment. A jungle environment training opportunity did finally arrive when we were directed by Department of the Army to perform evaluation of the Army's new rifle, the M-16 in the jungle. My company was selected to perform the required tests. Evaluators arrived and we conducted numerous firing exercises as well as testing the ability of the weapon to withstand the daily punishment of the high humidity, terrible heat, and intense rain showers during extensive jungle exercises. These tests and normal day-to-day operations continued until early 1963. Many of the officers and senior NCO's that took part in the test were not at all happy about the size of the .223mm bullet and its travel at very high velocity. They saw the bullet was deflected very easily by small branches. Conversely, the 30/06 bullet fired by the M1 and M14 rifles would plow through brush to the target. These and other concerns were all included in the test report.

In March 1963, I was notified that I would depart the Canal Zone and be reassigned to the states. I was to attend two schools: The Army Special Forces Officer School at Fort Bragg, North Carolina, and the Marine Corps School equivalent to the Army Advance Course. The Fort Bragg School was an indoctrination concerning the mission and concept of the Special Forces. These forces were designed to train and lead guerrilla forces anywhere in the world. All was going great until the final exercise. This was a weeklong exercise that began with a parachute jump into the exercise area. In preparation for this exercise we had packed everything we thought we would need in our rucksacks. They were then packed on pallets and were parachuted with us on the jump. When we landed on the ground, we would locate the pallets and be on our way. In the case of a small group of us, it did not work out that way. We could not locate the pallet with our gear. We walked and looked, but with no luck. The result was a week of rain and walking with no rain gear or no clean socks, no shaving with a razor, and very little sleep with no sleep gear. An exercise I am glad to forget.

The Marine School at Quantico, Virginia was a year in length, and the four Army officers that were attending were treated very well. I had no knowledge of the Army sending officers to the Marine School and was pleased with the opportunity. Once again, a beneficial decision in which my Lord had to have been involved because I certainly was not. There were two significant differences between the Marine course and the Army course. The Marines had no regimental or division size airborne units, hence there were no exercises where ground units had to coordinate with airborne units. All the Army officers had served in airborne units and were airborne qualified, so we had some interesting and heated discussions on this subject. The other difference was the requirement with the Marines to take a foreign language. I planned on taking Spanish, but something turned me to French. Our great

God knew I would have a need for French in less than a year. We had a wonderful year with the Marines but, as so many of you will recall, there was a war going on in South Vietnam. My new orders were to the United States Military Assistance Command in Vietnam. With these new orders, I packed up the family and headed back to Joliet where they stayed until my return a year later.

CHAPTER 5

VIETNAM TO SCHOOL FOR ADVANCE DEGREE

Traveling to Vietnam for the first time was a unique experience. We flew on a contract commercial aircraft from San Francisco to Saigon, Vietnam with one or two stops for refueling along the route. Upon departing the aircraft, we were met by administrative personnel who instructed us as to our future assignment and its location. I was notified I would be assigned as an advisor to the Vietnamese Airborne Brigade. I had no idea there was an airborne brigade in the Vietnamese Army and, if I did, I had no idea of how to get an assignment with them. Once again, our Lord was looking after me according to His plan for my life. He somehow gave me one of the best advisor assignments in all of Vietnam. I was transported to the brigade headquarters in Saigon and, subsequently, to the advisor offices. There I learned I would serve as senior advisor to the 7th Vietnamese Airborne Battalion located at Bien Hoa Air Base, about 20 miles north of Saigon. I would have one lieutenant and one senior NCO on the advisory team.

The brigade provided each senior advisor with a jeep and some directions, then I was on my way to Bien Hoa. Upon arrival, I eventually located the other 2 team members and was given a good rundown on the lay of the land around Bien Hoa. I set up a meeting with the Vietnamese battalion commander and his staff for the next day and talked with the lieutenant to feel out the Vietnamese before our meeting. I learned that the Vietnamese battalion commander, Thieu Ta Nhi (aka lieutenant colonel), had been fighting with the French throughout the French-Indo war and fighting against the Viet Cong for many more years. He had been wounded several times and his face was totally scarred. He spoke no English yet he was fluent in French. Now I could only hope the French language course I took with the Marines at Quantico would pay off. There was also Dai UyAihn (aka Captain) who was the S3 operations officer for the battalion. He spoke broken English, except when excited and then he could not be understood! Finally, there was the battalion surgeon who was a young captain and spoke very good English. I spent that evening preparing for my meeting with the Vietnamese.

Early the next day, the team and I headed for the battalion headquarters. The meeting was cordial and somewhat beneficial. I sensed that the battalion commander was looking me over and thinking about his 20 plus years in combat versus my big fat zero. After the meeting, I spoke briefly with the young surgeon and told him to tell the battalion commander that I was not here to run his command. I was here to ensure he receives the fire support, intelligence support, and medical evacuation support he needs when he needs it. The next afternoon, we were alerted that the battalion was to move out to the Delta in the Southern regions of South Vietnam. Our mission was to find and destroy a Viet Cong force that had killed 3 American advisors. I knew this would be a test of my ability of giving the needed support. We trucked to the general region and then started our foot movement. After several hours, we came to the place where the battle (which took the American lives) had been fought. Captain Aihn, the battalion operations officer, was talking to some local villagers and they said they knew where the Americans had died. As he started out with them, he called out for me to join him. The site was only a few hundred yards away but, when I saw the hundreds of expended

Photo #9: Vietnam Battalion Advisor 1964

cartridges in an area where the ground was covered with dried blood, I knew they had put up one hell of a fight. As gruesome as the site was, I said a short prayer for the families of each American and the South Vietnamese troops that were killed.

The battalion continued walking for another mile or so until the battalion point element engaged the Viet Cong unit. Two companies were quickly brought online and started their advance. I alerted the L-19 observation aircraft that was overhead that we needed helicopter UTT gunships immediately and to alert medevac that we will need their support. The gunships quickly arrived and provided outstanding fire support. This was my first experience at controlling helicopter gunships in combat. I think the pilots figured I was a newbie at directing close air support, so they helped a great deal. I would throw a smoke grenade a short distance and ask them to identify the color smoke. When they did, I would give them a distance from the smoke and a compass heading for the attack. Their first run down the compass heading would be with only a few short bursts of fire from a single machine gun. If the run was not endangering our troops, the next run was with all machine guns and rockets.

The battalion commander maneuvered one company to the Viet Cong flank, which forced the enemy to direct its fire toward these advancing troops. Another company moved down the slope of the ridge and forced the enemy to withdraw. The 2 rifle companies pursued the enemy and destroyed most of the enemy force. We spent the next few hours caring for the wounded and loading the more serious cases onto medevac helicopters. It was always heart-wrenching to see those young Vietnamese men so seriously wounded. Many were chattering in Vietnamese that I did not understand, but a smile and a pat on their shoulder seemed to help. When all the troops were cared for or transported out, I heard one of the medical soldiers yelling something in Vietnamese and this caused many of the soldiers that were not wounded to gather near the pile of stretchers.

Then came the real shock. The soldiers were urinating on the stretchers. I watched in dismay and, when I saw the surgeon, I asked him why the soldiers were doing that. He explained that they always did that to remove the blood so the medics could wash the stretchers with soap and water to get them ready for the next action. What I initially thought was terrible, now made sense. Afterward, we loaded trucks for the long trip back to Bien Hoa. This time provided me an opportunity to thank my Lord for keeping me from panicking when the first burst of enemy fire came in. To those who have never heard the sound, it is shocking. You are not only hearing the explosive sound of the weapons firing the bullets, but an even louder sound are the hundreds of enemy bullets that are passing you at the speed of sound; each bullet makes a significant cracking sound as it has broken the sound barrier. If you couple that with the sound of grenades exploding everywhere, you will have a significant hearing problem. I also came through with a great appreciation for the value of the ground and prayer!

An aside to the war and battles, for a few days, was an invitation by the Airborne Brigade for advisors to gain the Vietnamese Master Jump Wings. Until this offer, advisors to the brigade could gain the standard silver Vietnamese jump wings after several basic parachute jumps with their unit. To gain the Master Jump Wings, we had to do several free-fall jumps. The first jump was from 2000 feet while the normal jump altitude for standard jumps with a circular chute was 1200 feet. I had completed several hundred standard jumps without much trouble. On this, my first free fall I ran into a little trouble. I exited the helicopter in a controlled free-fall position and, after a standard delay count, pulled my main ripcord – nothing happened. I was waiting for the opening shock but felt nothing except the rushing air. My next action was to pull the reserve chute ripcord. The reserve chute literally exploded in opening at the speed I was falling. The important thing was, it opened, and then the main chute started to open. I was concerned that the main might wrap around the reserve, so I cut the main away with the 2 quick releases. Then I rode the reserve chute into landing. An exciting first sky dive! What had happened was called a "burble" in sky diving vernacular. When I pulled the main ripcord, the pilot chute that pulls the main into deployment was caught in the vacuum on my back and fluttered there because it could not catch enough air to deploy. I learned from this experience that, if there is a delay in the main opening, try bringing one arm in to turn the body slightly to break the vacuum at the pack tray.

Back to our job as advisors. During our initial orientation, we had been instructed that, whenever our battalion had a firefight or other contact with the enemy, we must brief the other advisors as soon as possible after our return. The next morning, I went to Saigon and conducted the briefing, and spent some time talking with the American intelligence analysts. They indicated there was more movement along the Ho Chi Minh trail and they would not be surprised if some of the airborne battalions might be sent to that region.

I departed Saigon and, upon my return to Bien Hoa, I informed the rest of our team about the intel and passed it on to the battalion S3. Thankfully, things were quiet for a week, but a week later, we were notified the battalion was alerted for movement to Quang Tri Province. That is the northern most province in South Vietnam. The battalion went through its normal routine for deployment. As advisors, we checked and cross-checked ammunition and emergency ration supplies for the unit. We also verified helicopter gunship support and procedures for employment in that province. Had we been working with standard Vietnamese infantry units, there would have been problems. Fortunately, the airborne units were so much more professional. We flew in C-130 aircraft from Bien Hoa to the military air base at Quang Tri. Upon arrival at Quang Tri, I met with some of the Province American advisors and they gave a good rundown on the area as well as what we could expect. The battalion began the very long trek to the west on a route just south of the Ben Hai River, which divides North and South Vietnam. We walked many miles and

Photo #10: Vietnam near Laotian border 1964

finally stopped for the evening. The next morning, we began the trek again and moved into Laos territory. For the next several weeks, we moved further into Laos. From the beginning, I knew I was in for some trouble. My stomach was giving me fits and there were gripping pains and diarrhea. I asked the surgeon about my problem and he gave me some pills. Unfortunately, the pills did not solve the problem. Forgive my candor, but it will make sense as we go along.

We continued moving and, eventually, as we climbed higher in the foothills, we came upon a large stream flowing rapidly down the mountainside. As evening approached, we stopped and set up security for the night. Suddenly, I heard explosions and moved to determine the source. What I saw were the cooks throwing grenades into the large puddles that had formed along the stream banks. When the grenades exploded, several fish came floating to the surface, and the cooks grabbed them for our evening meal. Now that was a different way to catch fish! After the meal, as darkness set in, the battalion medical doctor informed me of two men wounded earlier in the day. He wanted them medically evacuated, so I contacted the L-19 that was overhead and asked for a medevac chopper at first light. The night passed very quickly and, at first light, we were preparing to move out when I received a radio call from a Marine medevac helicopter. I informed the commander and the unit established security while I searched for a suitable landing site.

When I found what I thought was a good site, I threw a smoke grenade and guided in the helicopter. I had never given hand and arm signals to a Marine helicopter, but the landing went smoothly. After the wounded were loaded, I was about to signal the helicopter for takeoff when we started receiving enemy fire from ground positions below our location on the ridge. Our troops returned fire and started to maneuver against the enemy. The helicopter remained on the ground because the pilots did not want to take off and present a large airborne target for the enemy. I was moving to get a better view so I could employ gunships if they were needed. As I ran, the sound of enemy bullets passing close to me became louder, so I dove into a shallow embankment for cover. Unfortunately, I landed in an area where the enemy had installed numerous punji stakes. These stakes are made from dried bamboo and are sharpened to a point and, generally, heated to make them stronger and stiffer. Finally, they were treated with human feces or other contaminants and were partially buried in the ground so anyone attempting to take cover in that piece of low ground would be wounded or killed. I can thank my Lord and Savior that I was not killed, but I did have a significant problem. One of the stakes had entered my right calf and passed through the leg to exit in the knee area. As I laid there and attempted to stop the flow of blood, I signaled for Sergeant Maldonado. He came running and, when he saw my wound, he helped me to the helicopter.

I worried about leaving the unit because it left only Sergeant Maldonado, my senior NCO member of the team, as the only American advisor. Our team lieutenant had been killed in an earlier operation and a replacement had not arrived. I asked the Lord to watch over Sergeant Maldonado. Upon arrival at Quang Tri, the doctors removed the bamboo stake, pumped me full of penicillin, and sewed the wound. They were concerned about the wound, but also about my condition regarding weight loss. I did not realize it, but the doctors indicated I had anemic dysentery. I was down to 139 pounds versus a weight of about 170 pounds when we started the operation. They wanted to commit me to the hospital but, at my request, released me. The American advisor team for that region was most helpful and was able to hook me up telephonically with my headquarters in Saigon. I advised the colonel what had happened and was informed my battalion was heading back to Quang Tri for return to Bien Hoa. I waited and rejoined the unit at the airfield for the flight back to home base.

At home base, my wound was not improving. It was getting much worse with considerable swelling and pain. Our medical team committed me to the hospital primarily for my wound, but also for the anemic dysentery. A few days later, a doctor came to my bed. He said the tests indicated an infection, which could ultimately result in gangrene, had begun to settle in my leg. If it worsened and gangrene did start to settle, my leg would have to be amputated. He stated that the doctors that first handled the case should never have sewn up both ends of a puncture wound without proper drainage. To say I was shocked is an understatement. As the doctor left, I foresaw nothing but doom and gloom. Later that same day, a young medical major came to me and said he had heard about my leg and would like to try something he had read recently in a medical bulletin. I was all for anything that could save the leg. The major's solution consisted of bandages soaked in a special solution. They were to be applied to the leg wounds with very bright light just inches from the bandages. The light did more than light up the wound area; it also provided considerable heat. Shortly after the light was turned on, the bandage started to turn a blackish red color, and then the bandage was replaced with a new one, and on and on all day and night. They were also loading me with penicillin and morphine. In about two days, the major indicated they were seeing improvement, so he wanted to keep the process going for another few days. I certainly agreed but, to this day, I believe God sent that major to save my leg. He had other plans for my life. In another few weeks, I was released from the hospital and was told to take it easy a few weeks.

After my recovery, the Vietnamese Brigade ordered the battalion to move to a region in central Vietnam to work with a regular infantry battalion to clear a large rubber plantation area. These rubber plantations were products of the French influence and were present throughout the country. They were very neat rows of equally placed rubber trees several hundred yards in length. We joined the infantry battalion and, after some coordination, we began our movement into the rubber plantation. Sadly, we had no way of knowing that we were walking into an enemy ambush. Our battalion was on the north side of the only dirt road in the area, while the infantry battalion was on the south side. While we walked, I was talking to the battalion surgeon when we suddenly came under intense small arms fire from very close range. I returned fire immediately as I dove to the ground.

I was able to shoot the two closest enemy soldiers when my radio operator fell on me. I dragged him into a small ravine for cover from enemy fire. He had been standing right next to me and was shot in the shoulder, hip, and arm. He was losing a great deal of blood, so I applied pressure and tourniquets as I worked the radio to get gunships to help with the fight. I finally got the radio off his back and dragged it with me as I moved to get a better view of the total area. I was lying behind a rubber tree when I saw Dai Uy Aihn (the S3) a short distance away. He was using one of the rubber trees for cover and was pointing to enemy positions so that the soldiers on the ground could take them under fire. While I was looking at the Dai Uy, he was hit by a bullet that appeared to have entered under the pointing arm and exited with tremendous force through the opposite shoulder. His shoulder appeared to explode, and he immediately collapsed. The medics arrived to treat him in seconds, but he was dead.

In a few minutes, the first gunships arrived. I threw a smoke grenade and, when they identified the smoke, I gave them a heading and distance to cover with their machine guns and rockets. Suddenly, I saw two enemy soldiers and fired on them. Other enemy soldiers opened fire and several rounds hit the tree behind which I was lying. Fortunately, the bullets did not hit me directly. They ricocheted off the tree as fragments into my arm and side. By this time, our young Vietnamese airborne soldiers had advanced and cleared the area where the enemy had been firing. I am thankful to my heavenly Father that the enemy soldiers were not better shots. I bandaged the wounds as good as possible and was able to continue with the unit. My radio operator was not so fortunate.

The gunships were doing a super job and the medevac birds were flying overhead awaiting clearance to land. About this time, I called the advisor of the infantry battalion to see if they could sweep the left flank of the area where the enemy was located. He told me they had departed the area as soon as we came under fire and were at least two miles to the rear of the action. This action by the Vietnamese infantry unit did not surprise me. It made me angry because it endangered my unit, but it showed the significant difference between the airborne units and the infantry units. The infantry units were armed with M1 rifles that our Army abandoned years before. The airborne units, on the other hand, were equipped with the newest M16 rifles and their leaders were so much more attuned to the tactical situations. I always felt a pang of pity for the advisors of the infantry units.

I should point out a sidelight for this adventure. This action took place on a Sunday morning. I learned later that the helicopter gunship crews were awakened in such a rush for the mission that many were still in their PJ's and other sleepwear when they were flying the mission. I also want to note that I prayed a bunch during this relatively short period of battle. Thankfully, my holy Father was not ready for me at that time. The soldiers searched the area for any other enemy and we started our trek away from the area lacking many of our young soldiers who were killed or wounded.

There was considerable anguish and sorrow throughout the battalion area when we returned to Bien Hoa. The senior officers and NCOs knew they had walked into an enemy ambush, a severe tactical error. Every member of the command felt some shame and sorrow for the loss of so many men. I later learned that the battalion had employed flank security, but the unit providing this security was on the other side of the enemy when the fire fight started. When the funerals for the fallen were scheduled, I decided to attend the funeral for Dai Uy Aihn, the battalion operations officer. I recall he was lying in an open casket and I went up to the casket and kneeled to pray, but I obviously caused a minor stir among his wife and family. Thankfully, when I stood up, the surgeon came to me and asked me to speak to the family. The surgeon acted as interpreter and the wife and a few elders asked why an American would kneel at the casket. I told them I knelt to show respect and to offer some prayers for the family. They were extremely grateful and nice when I told them I thought Dai Uy Aihn was a very brave soldier. I learned from the family that he was

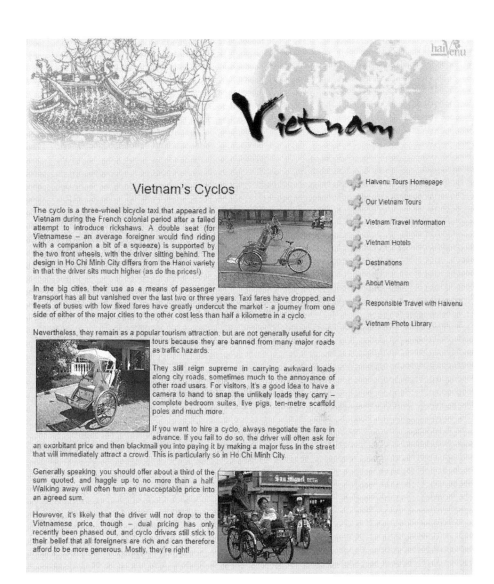

Vietnam's Cyclos

The cyclo is a three-wheel bicycle taxi that appeared in Vietnam during the French colonial period after a failed attempt to introduce rickshaws. A double seat (for Vietnamese – an average foreigner would find riding with a companion a bit of a squeeze) is supported by the two front wheels, with the driver sitting behind. The design in Ho Chi Minh City differs from the Hanoi variety in that the driver sits much higher (as do the prices!).

In the big cities, their use as a means of passenger transport has all but vanished over the last two or three years. Taxi fares have dropped, and fleets of buses with low fixed fares have greatly undercut the market - a journey from one side of either of the major cities to the other cost less than half a kilometre in a cyclo.

Nevertheless, they remain as a popular tourism attraction, but are not generally useful for city tours because they are banned from many major roads as traffic hazards.

They still reign supreme in carrying awkward loads along city roads, sometimes much to the annoyance of other road users. For visitors, it's a good idea to have a camera to hand to snap the unlikely loads they carry – complete bedroom suites, live pigs, ten-metre scaffold poles and much more.

If you want to hire a cyclo, always negotiate the fare in advance. If you fail to do so, the driver will often ask for an exorbitant price and then blackmail you into paying it by making a major fuss in the street that will immediately attract a crowd. This is particularly so in Ho Chi Minh City.

Generally speaking, you should offer about a third of the sum quoted, and haggle up to no more than a half. Walking away will often turn an unacceptable price into an agreed sum.

However, it's likely that the driver will not drop to the Vietnamese price, though – dual pricing has only recently been phased out, and cyclo drivers still stick to their belief that all foreigners are rich and can therefore afford to be more generous. Mostly, they're right!

Haivenu Tours Homepage
Our Vietnam Tours
Vietnam Travel Information
Vietnam Hotels
Destinations
About Vietnam
Responsible Travel with Haivenu
Vietnam Photo Library

Photo #11: Cyclos

a professor at the university and volunteered to leave the school to fight the Viet Cong.

After getting some rest and medical care, I went back to Saigon and briefed the advisors on the operation with considerable emphasis on the need to look at ambush prevention techniques. After my briefing, the colonel decided that two purple hearts were enough, so he was transferring me to the brigade staff in Saigon. I quickly learned that Saigon was a much different world than Bien Hoa. It was very much like a large American city during daylight hours. The streets were full of cyclos, three-wheel pedal driven devices where two passengers sat in front and the driver was behind them on what looked like a bicycle. Once the sun set, the number of bars that opened their doors was unbelievable. Almost every other building entrance led to a bar, and every bar offered numerous drinks and hundreds of young Vietnamese prostitutes.

I had served in Saigon for only two months and, thankfully, the good Lord came through with orders to attend the Command and General Staff College (CGSC) at Fort Leavenworth, Kansas. This one-year school is one of the steppingstones required for success in the Army. As I was about to leave Vietnam, I learned that the United States was sending American forces to fight the battle. I knew the secretary of defense and possibly the president were concerned about the domino effect of communism gradually taking over the entire Far East. Once again, the United States was going to war to defend a nation that was losing the war against the Viet Cong and would lose the war against the North Vietnamese. When we watch the news today, we obviously did not learn much from the Vietnam fiasco. I was just glad I made it out alive and headed for Joliet, Illinois to gather the family and drive them to Fort Riley, Kansas.

CHAPTER 6

COMMAND AND GENERAL STAFF COLLEGE TO VIETNAM

CGSC was a super break after Vietnam. We had several hundred officers in the grade of captain and major assigned to the class, and we learned a great deal and gained several new friends. JoAnn and I rented a very small house a short distance from the post. Fortunately, the house had a basement, which was occupied several times during tornado alerts. The boys enjoyed themselves in the new environment of Kansas. I was promoted to major while at the school and spent a great deal of time enjoying the relaxed atmosphere of the school environment. Unfortunately, the year did not last long enough. We were off to a new assignment at the Infantry Branch in Washington, D.C. This assignment caused the family some concern because there was no way to know how long we would be in the Washington area; hence, the question of, "Should we buy or rent?" Tom Runyan, a classmate from West Point, informed me that he had an empty house in Virginia he did not want to rent. He allowed JoAnn and I to occupy it while we house hunted. We were fortunate and found a great little brick house in Maryland just outside the beltway. We were riding back from looking at another house that was priced much too high. As we drove through a small subdivision in Maryland, we saw a "For Sale" sign in the yard of a very nice brick home, so we stopped. The lady who owned the home was very nice and quoted a price of $27,000 for the three-bedroom, small dining room, living room, decent sized kitchen, and a full finished basement. The price was reasonable, the location was great, and the kids' school was only three blocks away. We were convinced the good Lord had His hand in us finding that home. Many years later, a friend looked at this same house but thought the price of $175,000 was too high! When I told him what we had paid for the house, he gave up on that purchase.

After we moved into our Maryland home, I reported for duty at the Infantry Branch. My duties were primarily as the assignment officer for all Army infantry lieutenants. There were a great number of lieutenants that required assignments. Many days, I would bring the files home and spread them out on the ping-pong table. There were so many lieutenants that had just graduated from college ROTC. Because they were new, their file had hardly any information in them on which to base their assignment. I wanted to keep newly commissioned officers from going to Vietnam as their initial assignment. I hoped they could gain some experience in a unit in the states or in Europe before assuming command of a unit in combat. I was not completely successful with this endeavor. I continued assigning lieutenants for the next two years.

Following my work in Infantry Branch, I was given a great opportunity to attend graduate school at George Washington University for my master's degree in business administration and data processing; this was a two-year program. The family was especially happy because they could remain in the house in Maryland. Many of my classes were at night, so I decided to get a part-time job to gain additional income. I filled out part-time applications at several places and ended up at the Woodward & Lothrop department store. It was ideal because it was less than a mile from the house. Within a month after starting employment, the manager asked me to work full-time.

Next, he made me manager of the men's department. In this position, I quickly learned that the automation system in use by the store was very disjointed with little or no cross-feed between sales, marketing, and procurement. This led me to write my master's thesis on the use of automation in the retail environment.

One significant event on Christmas Eve caused a little excitement. The store was to close at 5:00 p.m. with a store party after closing. I stuck around for a few minutes, but left within a half hour to be home with the family. As evening approached, I received a call from the store manager. From his voice, I figured he was more than a little intoxicated. He asked if I locked the store. I explained I left at 5:30 and the party was just starting. He then asked if I would go to the store and check if the alarm was properly set. I agreed, hung up, and headed for my car. When I arrived at the store, everything initially looked correct but, when I tried the front door, it was not locked. I entered the store knowing I had only minutes before the alarm could go off. When I reached the alarm panel and was about to shut the system down, I found the alarm had never been set. I also noted the lights had not been turned off. I walked the first and second floor and noticed nothing out of the ordinary. I called the manager from one of the office phones and informed him of what I had found. I told him to relax since it was apparent that the good Lord was watching over the store on this Christmas Eve. With that, I shut off the lights, reset the alarm system, checked that all doors were properly locked, and headed home for the holidays.

When the two-year advance degree program ended, I was again reassigned to Vietnam. This time, on arrival in Saigon, I was assigned to the 1st Brigade, 5th Infantry Division that was operating in Quang Tri province, the most Northern Province in South Vietnam. I immediately recalled walking that same ground with the Vietnamese Airborne Battalion in that same province five years earlier. I flew up to Quang Tri and reported to the brigade commander who initially assigned me to a staff position to learn the idiosyncrasy of this separate brigade. Unlike interior brigades of a division, these separate brigades have their infantry and armor battalions, but also their own artillery battalion, support battalion, and numerous other small support elements. The brigade headquarters was in Quang Tri and the combat elements operated from fire bases throughout the region. The term "firebase" came about because there were no front lines in Vietnam as has been seen in more conventional wars. The firebase is comprised of numerous underground bunkers as well as above ground bunkers with 2 to 3 feet of dirt over and around each bunker. Then concertina razor wire was installed in depth around the perimeter as well as an extensive minefield. Two-man bunkers around the interior perimeter of the firebase were manned at night. These small bunkers had machine guns and claymore anti-personnel mines that were controlled by the soldiers in the bunkers. The firebase had a helipad for landing helicopters and may possess artillery weapons for indirect fire when the units of the firebase were operating in the area around the firebase.

One evening, as I was going over some reports that had to be submitted to Saigon, I was called to the Brigade Operations Center. There I was briefed that a platoon-sized force from the 61st Infantry Battalion was heavily engaged with enemy forces. The platoon had been sent out to establish an ambush position to stop enemy infiltration through that area. Through the radio interceptions, it was apparent that some enemy forces had determined the location of the platoon and had somehow crawled so close to the platoon firing positions that they were able to turn the claymore mines so that they faced the platoon positions. The Claymore mine is a rectangular explosive device about 4 inches high and 9 inches long. It contained high explosive and hundreds of small metal balls and was mounted on a small plastic tripod. It had a long pair of wires that went from the mine to the soldier that placed it. At the end was a plastic trigger device to set the weapon off. It was a very effective killing machine. The enemy soldiers that had crawled up to turn the mine around subsequently opened fire on the platoon positions. This led the platoon to return fire and set off the Claymore mines. The result was that numerous platoon soldiers were wounded or killed, and the battle continued as additional enemy forces arrived in the area. The artillery units located on the closest firebase opened fire and were successful in driving the enemy from that location. At first light, we brought medevac helicopters in for the wounded and transported the dead to Quang Tri. Some very sad lessons were learned that night and we prayed that they would not be repeated. My heart was heavy because these young soldiers were draftees and they died primarily because of a lack of sound leadership from the officers and NCO's of the unit.

After a month on the staff, I was given command of the 1st Battalion, 61st Infantry. It is the parent unit of the company that provided the platoon described in the previous paragraph. The battalion operated from firebase Charlie 2 (C2) and Alpha 4 (A4). The northern firebase was A4 and was located just south of the Ben Hai river that separated South and North Vietnam. This was the northern most American position in South Vietnam. The change of command ceremony was held on firebase C2 where the battalion headquarters was located. C2 was about a half mile south of A4. A change of command ceremony normally includes the entire battalion on parade, but we reduced the size to one platoon of about 30 men. The reason was obvious because, as the change of command orders were being announced, enemy rocket fire was launched from rocket ridge and everyone scurried for cover. Fortunately, all the rockets exploded harmlessly and caused no injuries or damage. The 155mm and 8" artillery batteries on C2 immediately returned fire and life went back to normal. I should emphasize that both firebases had lived through extensive rocket and mortar fire over the previous years. The facilities where the soldiers slept, where they stood security around the base perimeter, where the vehicles were maintained, and every place the soldiers were required to be were all underground or covered bunkers.

Photo #12: Vietnam as battalion commander 1970

After the change of command, I assembled the company and battery commanders in our large mess bunker to start a dialogue on how to improve our day-to-day operations. Some offered good ideas and some not so great, but we developed some plans and schedules for implementation. I wanted to keep two company-sized forces outside the firebase every day. They would maneuver in those areas where intelligence indicated the enemy infiltration was taking place. Each day, I flew in a small observation helicopter (OH-58) over the maneuvering companies and landed if I saw a need to talk to the commander privately. I often had the commander take the helicopter to observe his anticipated route of movement. If the weather was not good for flying, I would take my M-113 Command Vehicle and move with the companies.

A concern that I held about many of the firebases throughout Vietnam was the age and condition of the mines, barbed wire, and other security devices spread around the position. Some firebases were several years old and had undergone numerous monsoon rains that could have significant effect on the ground and the buried mines. This concern and several others caused me to make nightly walks of the security perimeter. It gave me an opportunity to talk with numerous young soldiers of the battalion. During these sessions, I learned that the drug problems of the unit were much larger than I imagined. I became an expert at the smell of marijuana and had to have numerous soldiers replaced on the security bunkers because they were so impaired from the drugs that they could never be trusted with the security of the base. As an example, when a soldier is questioned as to how to detonate the Claymore mines in front of his position, he gave a completely erroneous reply.

A significant problem the units faced every day was the presence of North Vietnamese anti-tank mines. These were installed at night by the enemy in areas where they thought our armored vehicles would travel. These were nuisance mines. They were buried at night and left for the future. Our tanks encountered many of these mines and they would break the tanks' track, but would not penetrate the hull. The M-113 personnel carriers were more susceptible to severe damage by these mines. If an M-113 ran over a mine, the explosion would normally rip the floor enough to send shrapnel into the interior wounding or killing many of the soldiers inside. In one case an M-113 ran over a mine with its right track which exploded flipping the vehicle on its side. The side landed on what we think was a stacked pair of mines which destroyed the vehicle and killed every soldier in the vehicle. We used specially trained dogs, mine detectors, and spades on the front of the M113's but we could never overcome the problem.

One afternoon, while flying over the companies near the Ben Hai river, the operations center at our headquarters radioed to inform me that a soldier had departed from A4 and it appeared he was proceeding north toward the river. He was armed with his M-16 rifle and his fellow soldiers said he was acting very strangely stating something about getting out of Vietnam. I made a radio call to request an immediate HU1 helicopter for an emergency. We flew back to A4 and transferred to the larger HU1 helicopter. While we took off, I explained to the pilot and crew what was happening and we started our search just north of A4 and searched to the north. After a few minutes, we saw the soldier walking in a large field. I had the pilot fly directly over the soldier, yet at an altitude that I could jump from the chopper and hopefully stop him from going any farther north. The pilot flew just 10 feet off the ground, so I jumped and landed just behind the young man. I grabbed the M-16, threw it aside, and wrestled him to the ground while the chopper landed and the door gunners assisted in subduing the soldier. He kept screaming that he was going home and had to get out of Vietnam. After talking to him several minutes, I was able to convince him that he should board the chopper and we would go directly to Quang Tri hospital. We boarded the helicopter and delivered the young soldier to the hospital. The Army presented me with a soldiers medal for this action so I submitted a request that the pilots and door gunners deserved similar awards. I had left the battalion before those awards were presented.

Another helicopter incident took place with an OH-58 helicopter near the Ben Hai river when I was observing the advance of one of our rifle companies. We were at about 500 feet altitude when we were hit by enemy fire. Several rounds penetrated the fuselage and 1 or 2 struck the pilot in his right leg and side. Several rounds penetrated the instrument panel and caused alarms to sound off. I could see the pilot was losing a great deal of blood, so I unfastened my harness, removed my belt, and applied a tourniquet. I then assumed control of the chopper because the pilot was losing consciousness. Gratefully, I had learned to fly the bird on a level flight, but this was so much different. All the caution lights on the console were flashing as were several buzzers sounding. I knew that I somehow had to set the bird down, but we were very close to North Vietnam and the probability of enemy forces in the area was too high. Gradually, I nosed the bird down and lowered the cyclic. It was still going too fast. I tried to pull the cyclic while remembering to push the left pedal hard to avoid a spin. This is about where God stepped in and helped me land the helicopter. We hit very hard and the tail broke off, but the body remained in one piece. I jumped out and ran around the bird to lift the pilot out and laid him a few yards away from the helicopter. I told the door gunner to take the machine gun up the hill a short distance and cover us. He said he was out of ammo, so I gave him my rifle and said to stay close.

It was then that I heard the wonderful sound of M-113's moving fast toward my location. It was A Company and they quickly provided a perimeter security so we could call in a medevac bird for the pilot. Then a second Huey landed, and the pilot said he was to fly me to headquarters. I had forgotten the brigade was hosting the Vietnamese Vice President and the commanders were all supposed to be there. I had also forgotten that this day was Christmas Eve. There I was, quite dirty, and very sweaty going to a social event. Vietnam was a strange war. The Lord was good to me that day and, although the pilot lost his leg, we were all so very fortunate that God pulled us through.

Some days later, I was taking care of paperwork when the S3 called and asked me to come to the operations center because they had a major problem. What had happened is so sad, but all too true. A night patrol of seven men had departed the operations center after having been briefed on their mission. The normal procedure for all such patrols was to go down a specified path until they had cleared the perimeter barbed wire and minefield. This patrol had walked down the path but turned before going beyond the barbed wire and minefield. They had entered the mine field and, shortly after entering, one of them tripped a bouncing mine that expelled a high explosive canister about waist high and then detonated, killing or wounding everyone, including the patrol leader. It was pitch black when the incident took place. We had to move and could not wait for daylight. I sent for engineers and alerted another rifle company. We briefed the engineers on the situation and told them to enter the minefield and by probing clear a path wide enough to the patrol so that we could drag the dead and wounded out the cleared area. We gave them some infantrymen to drag the dead and wounded out while they cleared the area around each wounded or dead soldier. As the dead soldiers were pulled from the minefield, we placed them in body bags and put them on trucks for movement to Quang Tri. The wounded were immediately loaded on two medevac helicopters and flown to the Quang Tri hospital. More very sad letters of condolence that had to be written to wives and parents.

One more incident took place as my tour in Vietnam was about to end. I was in my bunker when I heard someone coming down the stairs. I looked up to see a young soldier pulling a fragmentation grenade from his belted ammo pouch. He was yelling something, but I was only interested in what he had in his hand. I moved to his side and grabbed his hand with both of my hands. Now we had a live grenade with the pin pulled and the only thing preventing it from exploding was our hands clamped around the grenade so that the safety lever could not release. I began yelling. A major and several soldiers came running down the stairs. They knew immediately what was happening and several more hands wrapped around my hands and the young soldiers' hands. For the next many minutes, I and the other soldiers talked to the young soldier. Eventually, we were able to convince him that we would get him to a hospital. We could not find the grenade pin, so I told one of the soldiers to get a paper clip from my field desk and straighten it so it would act as the grenade pin. With that, one more Vietnam incident was over. The young soldier was held under guard until morning and then was evacuated to Quang Tri for treatment. I learned later that he had been sent to a hospital in the Philippines.

Our battalion witnessed numerous visitors since we were the northern most military unit in South Vietnam. One important visitor was Admiral John S. McCain. He was the commander of the entire Pacific Command with station in Hawaii. We would receive notice that the admiral was coming for a visit a day or two before his expected arrival. We knew his visit was not an inspection. It was for personal reasons because his son, John McCain Jr. who later became a United States senator, was being held as a prisoner of war in North Vietnam. His aircraft had been shot down over North Vietnam and that resulted in his status as a prisoner. When the admiral arrived, we flew him to A4 where we had a bunker top prepared with a chair and a small table with water. We also had a bunker on a bunker so he could crawl into it if A4 took incoming rounds. He would sit on that bunker and look across the Ben Hai river into North Vietnam for several hours and then be flown out for his return to Saigon and then Hawaii. We also had visits from the Secretary of the Army and numerous other dignitaries who probably wanted to tell everyone they looked over the Ben Hai river into North Vietnam.

Photo #13: Admiral McCain Father of Senator McCain on C2 1971

CHAPTER 7

4TH INFANTRY DIVISION AND GERMANY

I felt very fortunate that my tour in Vietnam was about to end. Those that served in Vietnam or more current tours of duty in Afghanistan, Iraq, and Syria were fortunate in most cases to only spend a single year, and then head back home. When we think of the soldiers of WWII, we cannot comprehend overseas duty until the war was won. We always must hold those veterans in a special place in our hearts.

I was somewhat shocked when my order for reassignment arrived. They read that I was reassigned to the Computer Systems Command at Fort Belvoir in Virginia. It was a peculiar assignment for an infantry officer, but it was to meet the requirement that every officer must serve a utilization tour relative to the major of his master's degree. With my pending departure from Vietnam, I arranged for JoAnn to meet me in San Francisco and, from there, we would fly to Las Vegas for a short three-day vacation. Then our plan was to fly to Dulles International Airport in Virginia where JoAnn had left our car and, from there, a short drive home. The kids had been left at the house with JoAnn's sister's daughter who was watching over them. The flight from Vietnam was on a contract civilian airline from the Air

Force airfield near Da Nang Vietnam. One of our OH-58 helicopters picked me up at firebase C2 after a quick change of command and flew me to Da Nang. There I learned that my originally scheduled flight had been overbooked, so I was assigned to a flight that was scheduled for take-off a half hour later. I was concerned that a much later arrival would impact our scheduled flight from San Francisco to Las Vegas. Thankfully, the pilot must have felt my concern because he put the pedal to the metal and arrived at the same time as the original flight. I ran to the gate of the original flight and found JoAnn observing the passengers as they left the plane. I surprised her by sneaking up behind her and asking, "Are you looking for me?"

We made the flight to Las Vegas without difficulty and took a cab to Caesar's Palace to sign for our room. As I was signing us in, we heard a large commotion near the entrance to the hotel and one of the hotel managers approached us and asked that we come to his office. As we walked briskly toward his office, he explained that the noise was from an anti-Vietnam war group and they habitually harassed anyone in uniform. He went on to indicate that they had spit on soldiers in uniform and threw rotten tomatoes at them. I should mention that soldiers were required to wear their green uniform with dress shirt and tie for the flight from Vietnam; hence, I was in uniform. We sat in the manager's office for about 45 minutes and he returned to tell us that the way was now clear. It was unfortunate that the soldiers who were ordered by the leaders of our nation to fight that ridiculous war were harassed by their countrymen for doing their job.

On a brighter side, the family was very happy about this assignment because it allowed us to stay in our Maryland home. It was an interesting assignment but, after a year, I was pleased with new orders to an Army staff position in the Pentagon. While serving on the Army staff, our family grew by one with the birth of our daughter, Margaret (Peg). JoAnn and I were thrilled to have a pretty little lady in the family. Like Tom, Peg also suffered with changes to high school every year. As a teenager, Peg became an avid horse rider at Fort Bragg. She later attended college in Texas and began a teaching career. She married David Honaker and they have three very super children.

I was pleased with this tour in the Pentagon because I was able to apply some of the data automation techniques I had learned in my advanced degree. Now, when I compare the software of those days to that which is available today, we were way behind the power curve. I have written many times herein that the good Lord guided so many things in my life. One more was my next assignment as a student at the National War College. In order to progress to the senior ranks of the military, every senior officer must be selected to attend one of the service war colleges. I was very fortunate to be selected for this war college. The family was thrilled because the college is located at Fort McNair in Washington, DC, which meant another year in the Maryland home. From a professional perspective, this college provided opportunities to attend daily with men from numerous government agencies to include State Department, CIA, Energy, etc. It also included a month-long trip to Libya, Turkey, Afghanistan, Pakistan, India, Bahrain, Saudi Arabia, Jordan, and Israel. In each country, we met with the head of state and government principles to discuss potential issues of the future. Of interest to me was the issue of energy independence since the topic I had selected for my thesis was the energy problems of the early 1970's.

Upon completion of the war college, I received reassignment orders as operations officer (G3) for the 4th Infantry Division at Fort Carson, Colorado. I was thrilled with the news because I was going back to serving in an infantry unit on a post about which I had heard so many good things. Also, serving as G3 of a division was the optimum of staff assignment. Ironically, shortly after receiving the orders, I was called by the current division chief of staff. He informed me that I would not be the G3, but instead would be assigned as the Director of Personnel and Community Affairs (DPCA). This certainly took the air out of my balloon, so I decided to take some action myself. I went to the Chief of Infantry Branch and passed on the information.

The chief immediately contacted the 4th Infantry Division chief of staff and informed him that the orders stand as written or he would reassign me to a different unit. I left the office hoping things were back on track, but also thinking that God had again been involved with my future.

We finally had to leave the little brick house in Maryland but, before we could leave, I flew to Colorado Springs, Colorado, the city just outside Fort Carson, to look over the housing market. I found a new subdivision just a few miles from Fort Carson and purchased a new home. When I returned to Maryland, the family was ready to depart the little brick house in which they had lived over 6 years. In the military, 6 years in one house is wonderful and rare. We were very fortunate to sell it quickly and, ironically, it was sold to a West Point classmate. We left Maryland for Colorado in 2 cars and, after a brief stop to see our folks in Illinois, we decided that driving 2 cars was too much. We found a driving service and gave them the little Volkswagen to drive to Colorado. We drove the station wagon pulling our pop-up camping trailer. Everyone was happy when we arrived at our new home in Colorado Springs. The next week, I reported to the division commander and was welcomed as the new G3 of the division. As G3, I was kept quite busy on training and budgetary constraints. Reductions in military budgets in the 1970's had a significant impact on the training of a highly mechanized force since fuel and maintenance were very high-cost items. After serving as G3 for a little over a year, I was transferred to be the assistant chief of staff.

Duty as an assistant chief of staff was not high on my priority assignments, but it allowed me to learn a great deal about the operations of the post. In a situation where there is a single division on a post, the chief of staff serves the double role for the division and for the post. The post of Fort Carson has its own schools, a very large commissary (same as a very large Publix or Kroger), and a large post exchange (same as a large department store), a large hospital, plus a post office, and numerous other functions. The post has a separate staff that looks after post-type functions and reports to the chief of staff.

A few months later, the chief of staff was given command of one of the brigades. This meant a new chief had to be appointed. I waited anxiously for the announcement for which I would be working. To make matters even more confusing, it was announced that the division commander was being reassigned; therefore, a new commanding general would be assigned. The normal practice would be for the new commander to select his chief of staff; many new division commanders bring their own with them.

The commanding general surprised me when he walked in my office and informed me that I was the new chief of staff. I was more than a little nervous about the decision. What I did not know at the time was that the incoming division commander had called the current commander and indicated he would be bringing the new chief of staff. Had I known that fact, I would have been a little more nervous. Several weeks later, the new division commander, General Vessey, arrived at Fort Carson and was coming to the headquarters for the first time. As chief of staff, I waited on the steps of the headquarters. When the general arrived, I saluted and announced, "Colonel Scholtes, Chief of Staff, welcome to the 4th Division Sir." His response was a cold, "Don't you mean *Lieutenant* Colonel, Chief of Staff?" Oh, what a lousy way to start. Then, to top it off, this new commanding general was to be my immediate supervisor for several more years in a different environment and would have serious impact on my future in the Army.

Sometime later, I was promoted to colonel and was to given command of the 2nd Brigade. I was thrilled with that news. The 2nd Brigade had two infantry and one armored battalion. I envisioned numerous training events that I hoped could be applied to the units of the brigade. The restricted fuel availability and the cost of the fuel put the brakes on several of my ideas. As we studied alternatives for training, we learned that the division had been tasked to form a new separate brigade for transfer to Germany. One of the 2nd Brigade Infantry battalions was designated as a part of this new brigade. We also heard that an infantry battalion was also designated from the 1st Infantry division. There was considerable talk about this new outfit. Many wanted to know if they could transfer to the brigade because they wanted to go to Germany. Others wanted to know what it meant that some of the units of the new brigade would be serving on a TDY (temporary duty status) basis. As a separate brigade, this new organization would consist of a brigade headquarters, two infantry battalions, 1 tank battalion, 1 artillery battalion, 1 support battalion, a cavalry troop, and an engineer company. The brigade headquarters and support battalion were to be assigned on a permanent basis which normally meant three-year tours for the soldiers. All the remaining units were to be assignment on a TDY status, which meant the entire unit would be rotated back to the states in six months and be replaced by another unit of the same type.

The division staff was busy getting as many answers as they could, but questions kept coming. Then, much to my surprise, one afternoon the CG informed me that I was to form the new brigade. My immediate question was, "Who would assume command of the 2nd Brigade which I currently commanded?" The CG said words to the effect, "You can command both until you deploy." The next several months were somewhat hectic. In the morning, work with the 2nd Brigade and, in the afternoon, the 4th Brigade. To complicate the situation even more was establishing the training program for the battalion from Fort Riley when we had no idea as to their training status. Things were really getting messy.

Thankfully, the time had passed and we designated a day when the 2nd Brigade would have a change of command ceremony and, immediately thereafter, the 4th Brigade would have an activation ceremony. It all worked out well in the division, but there were many personal affairs that required some work. The families were not allowed to travel with the unit. The battalions on TDY status would not have their families join us in Germany. The remainder of the brigade would be advised when families could travel. Then came the question as to where these families would be housed.

I had never served in Germany, so I was very interested in where the brigade would be stationed, where families would be quartered, and where close in training areas could be found. I was informed that the brigade was moving into Wiesbaden Air Force Base, which had been the home of the Air Force Europe Headquarters. It was a short distance from Frankfurt. The Air Force had moved their headquarters to another area. We were told we could not use the runway for anything, but especially could not allow any vehicles (wheeled or tracked) on the runway. It was made of a new material that could easily be damaged from tires or tracks. Another problem concerned the housing for the troops. Several of the buildings to be used as troop billets had been office workspaces. There was considerable construction modification in order.

The time had come for me to leave Fort Carson and my family and depart for Germany. The flight over was without any incident and everyone was thankful for that. We had an impressive greeting at the airfield in Germany. The commanding general of all US forces in Germany was there as well as the commanding generals of all the allied nations to include the British, French, German, Belgium, and several others. It was quite an affair, but the members of the brigade were about worn out and needed some rest. The commanding general of the 8th Infantry Division pulled me aside and told me he would oversee the training of the brigade and, as such, the cavalry troop of our brigade would report daily to the Calvary squadron commander, and the artillery battalion commander would report to the 8th Infantry Division artillery commander, the Engineer company would report to the 8th ID Engineer battalion. I disagreed with these decisions so, that afternoon, I contacted the aide of General Blanchard, the commanding general of USAREUR. I explained that I needed to talk to the general about the brigade and a serious problem with the commanding general of the 8th Infantry Division. I was fortunate that I had served with General Blanchard as a lieutenant and he had come to my rescue in the past.

The aide put the general on and I explained the problem. The general told me not to worry, that he would make the necessary calls to take care of the situation. He did, but it took a long time to gain any relationship with the CG of the 8th. It was obvious he was convinced I would go to higher authority anytime I did not like his decision. I never went to higher authority again but, whenever he had a meeting with commanders in his office, he would state, "Colonel Scholtes, you can sit in that chair – the disloyal chair."

About two months later, the family flew to Germany after going through the pain of selling the house and arranging storage of our furniture and arranging transport of those items we would need. There was also the need to bring everything associated with the school records to ensure there would be no problems with entering the schools in Germany. While the brigade kept everyone very busy, we did have some free time to see and enjoy Germany. The whole family took a Thanksgiving Day trip to Zermatt, Switzerland to do some skiing, which was a wonderful time for everyone. We drove the car to a train station near the base of the mountain range and then had a unique train ride up the mountain. Of course, we had all that ski equipment for the three kids and me (JoAnn did not ski), skis, boots, poles, plus our luggage. We stayed in the nicest Swiss Chateau for the three nights. Another unique experience was the scenic boat tour on the Rhine River. The brigade staff and commanders with their wives all enjoyed the trip. The numerous castles along the Rhine were illuminated and very impressive and beautiful. We docked at one of the castles and were given a guided tour.

One afternoon the Support Battalion commander came to me concerning a unique find that he had just learned about. Apparently, a German construction company was excavating for a new building

Photo #14: Halftrack rebuilt by our support Battalion 1977

near Frankfurt and came across a buried American halftrack vehicle from WWII. This type vehicle was used extensively in armored units during the war. It was lightly armored, had two wheels in front for steering, and a track system where the rear wheels would normally be. The commander asked if he could retrieve the vehicle and spend spare time trying to get it back to running condition. I gave him the go-ahead, which eventually led to a well-restored halftrack that was used in future changes of command.

The brigade had the mission on the defensive line designed to stop the Soviet Union if they launched an attack. That mission meant the battalions and our headquarters spent a great deal of time designing the defensive plans. These plans had to be briefed to the corps commander on the ground of the defense line at least every other month. We identified a problem concerning ammunition resupply if the Soviet Union were to mass a major attack. As we worked through other problems, one of the battalion commanders came up with an idea concerning missile and ammunition resupply. His idea was to move large quantities of anti-tank missiles and tank gun ammunition as soon as a potential threat was apparent. This ammunition would be downloaded to farm buildings immediately to the rear of our defensive positions. We had a team of officers from the support battalion to reconnoiter the possible farm storage sites and, subsequently, I went to each farm with an interpreter and was able to gain their concurrence to use their outbuildings for such storage. We arranged to have the buildings reinforced and somewhat protected from enemy fire. Just when I was completely satisfied that we were ready for anything, I received one of those "are you for real" phone calls.

The call was from USAREUR headquarters informing me that new orders had been issued for my return to the States for assignment to the Military Academy at West Point. These orders were not what I had planned because I had only been in Germany for one year and had been told my next assignment would be to the headquarters in Heidelberg. It was a shock and I could not imagine why I was being reassigned to the United States Military Academy in less than a month. I did some checking and learned that a cheating or honor scandal had taken place at the academy and a commission known as the "Borman Commission" had been investigating. In their findings, they indicated the commandant of cadets was being pulled away from his commandant duties so often that he was not spending enough time dedicated to the cadets. One of the commissions fixes was to add a new colonel position as brigade tactical officer to manage many of the cadet issues concerning discipline and conduct. That was the position I was to fill. I could not find any specific information about the duties of the new position, so figured I would find out in due time. But first, I had to get the family moved to West Point.

CHAPTER 8

WEST POINT AND THE 82ND AIRBORNE DIVISION

I turned over command of the brigade, arranged for the car to be shipped, and the family finally flew from Frankfurt, Germany to New York City. We rented a car for the drive to West Point and, upon arrival at the academy, we were assigned housing. We were now ready to arrange having our household goods that were in storage in Colorado shipped to West Point. Eventually, the furniture and the car arrived, and things were back to normal. I had to learn what was expected in this new job as brigade tactical officer. This meant lengthy talks with Brigadier General Bard, the commandant of cadets. In addition to my position as the new brigade tactical officer, there were new lieutenant colonel regimental tactical officers for each of the four regiments, and captain or major company tactical officers to oversee all cadets within their company. There had been many more changes over the 20 years since I graduated. A significant change was the addition of female cadets, which required many changes to outdated procedures. One such change was due to the physical size of the female population wherein the commandant was forced to discontinue the age-old practice of sizing the cadet companies.

This sizing was designed to enhance camaraderie by having all cadets of a given height assigned to the same company. This sizing procedure also enhanced the appearance of the corps of cadets on parade on the large grassy parade ground, which was slightly sloped so. By sizing the companies, the shorter companies, called runts, were on the higher ground and the taller companies, called flankers, were on the lower ground. This arrangement gave a much-enhanced appearance of the formation. One can imagine how a unit of 60 cadets would look if many cadets were over 6 feet tall and the remainder were 4 to 5 feet tall. By eliminating the sizing, the corps of cadets looked much less military. The cadets also looked less military during parades because many of the female cadets had difficulty with a military marching pace. The length of the female step was so much shorter than the males that the women seemed to be out of step with the other cadets. Another thing that looked less military was the full-dress coats on female cadets. The male cadets' full dress coats had tails but, when I observed the female cadets in full-dress coats, there were no tails. The rationale for not having tails on the female dress coats was lame. All cadet uniforms are produced at a uniform manufacturing building on the West Point grounds. The representative from this facility informed me that the female dress coats had no tails because the shape of the female body made manufacturing dress coats more expensive. I would not buy that argument and called a meeting of the head staff of the uniform plant. At that meeting, I had two black male cadets with very large posteriors and one female cadet wear their full-dress coats and white trousers. We had a lengthy discussion and, when I had the cadets do an about face and face the wall, it was apparent the female posterior showed brightly in the white trousers versus the male cadets. We ended up agreeing that the female coats could and would be modified with tails. Win a few and lose a few such as the significant change of the cadet honor system. In the past, the honor system was managed solely by the cadets and it worked well. Lawyers have now been added to the system, which, in my opinion, was a terrible mistake.

Even with these and other changes, I was looking forward to two or three years as the brigade tactical officer. My God apparently did not agree with my assumptions because, at the end of my first year the superintendent called to inform me I had been selected for promotion to brigadier general. This was great news, but it meant I had to leave West Point. The family was not very anxious to make another move, and our kids had already been to two different high schools. The General Officer Management Office (GOMO) in the Pentagon also called to inform me that the promotion board wanted those officers who were on the promotion list and had not served in joint assignments where they were working on a day-to-day basis with members of the other services, to be moved to such an assignment. As a result, my new assignment was as a Deputy Director of Operations (DDO) in the National Military Command Center (NMCC). As DDO, you commanded the NMCC in the Pentagon on an eight-hour shift basis. The DDO was the manager of all crisis. Depending on the severity of the crisis, he would notify the appropriate leadership to include the secretary of defense and the president.

Before I could move onto this new assignment, I had to attend what the Army refers to as the "charm school." This is a course of instruction designed to assist the new general officers in making the transition from a specialist in one branch to a generalist in all branches of the service. I also had to attend Harvard University for courses associated with international relations. While I was undergoing these courses, JoAnn had to arrange our move from West Point to a new house we found in Virginia some distance from the Pentagon. I was able to squeeze in some leave to help the family with the move. This move required Tom to, once again, register for a new high school a third time in three years and Peg was going on two changes in the same time frame.

After getting somewhat settled in our new house, I reported for my assignment as DDO. There was a great deal of reading required concerning the procedures and duties. I was learning the many aspects of this new position and thought all was going very smoothly until, one morning, a 4:00 a.m. phone call notified me of a significant nuclear accident, a partial meltdown of reactor number 2 of Three Mile Island Nuclear Generating Station in Dauphin County, Pennsylvania, near Harrisburg. It was the most significant accident in U.S. commercial nuclear power plant history. As soon as I was called and informed of the situation, I notified the secretary of defense and the chairman of the Joint Chiefs of Staff. One of the requirements from the incident site was for helicopters to transport large panels of lead from storage sites to Three Mile Island. When I asked about the weight of the panels, they said a couple tons for each. I informed them we had no choppers available immediately to lift such a load, but we would get with the Army who synchronizes defense support of civil authority. They would provide truck lift support. The Army did a superb job in getting the trucks to the storage site and delivering the lead panels to the Three Mile Island site. The panels were required to shield reactor number 2. For many weeks, the NMCC and the Army continued to support the incident.

Another dramatic incident occurred while I was on duty on November 18, 1978. The events leading up to the incident and the incident itself were very hard to believe. The result was the death of over 900 of the members of the Peoples Temple Agriculture in Jonestown, Guyana in South America. It was commonly referred to as the "Jonestown Massacre." When I took the first phone call referencing the situation, I had difficulty grasping what had happened. Jim Jones, the Peoples Temple Agricultural Project leader, had somehow convinced his American followers that they were to drink from a cup. As they filed by, they were handed a cup of what many reported was Kool-Aid, but other reports indicated powdered milk laced with cyanide. The people then walked a short distance before they fell and died. With this information, I notified the secretary of defense and he told me to inform the president. I contacted the White House and I apprised the president of all the information we had. Military personnel were immediately deployed to the site in Jonestown. They began the gruesome task of separating the bodies and placing them in body bags or coffins. The soldiers described the scene as unbelievable with dead bodies to include many children strewn about and lying on top of each other. One can only imagine the carnage with 900 bodies in a small area. There were insufficient body bags in inventory, so coffins had to be purchased and deployed. The soldiers who were assigned this terrible duty indicated they will never forget forcing bloated bodies into the coffins.

My tenure as DDO was set at one year and, as the end of the year approached, I received a call from General Meloy, the commanding general of the 82nd Airborne Division. He informed me I was being assigned to the division as the Assistant Division Commander for Operations (ADCO). This came as a complete shock because I had left the division for my assignment in Panama as a new 1st Lieutenant way back in 1960, and now I was returning as a general officer in 1979. To say I was thrilled is a big understatement. ADCO of the only Airborne Division in the Army was the best job for which any infantryman could ask. When I examined everything that led up to this assignment, all my thanks go to my God. When I told the family that evening, Tom and Peg both shouted out, "Not another change of school!" There was also the problem of what to do with the house. After some deliberations, we decided to rent the house in case I was reassigned to the Pentagon in a few years.

The move to Fort Bragg went smoothly. This time the family was provided with a very nice, large house. What a difference from 20 years earlier! When the family was partially settled, I had to sign in at the division. I was required to undergo an airborne refresher course since it had been so long since my last airborne assignment. I had forgotten how sore a body could be after a week of swing landing trainers and 34-foot tower cable slides. After the airborne refresher training, I spent some time being briefed by each brigade and the headquarters so I could appreciate where each of the units stood regarding training and any problems with which they needed some help. Duty as the ADCO was both interesting and challenging. The commanding general gave considerable latitude in making recommendations concerning tactical and administrative procedures. I was committed to improve and enhance the marksmanship training in the division. I wanted to expand from what we learned in the evaluation of the M-16 rifle in Panama. Unfortunately, this effort had to be curtailed because a major event took place as I ended my first year with the division.

It was September 1979 and I had just completed the morning run. General Meloy, the division commander, came in my office and told me the chief of staff would be calling me in a few minutes. I mistakenly thought he was talking about the division chief of staff, so I was about to leave my office and go to the chief of staff office to see what he wanted when my phone rang. I picked it up to hear words to the effect, "Dick this is Shy Meyer (the 4-star Army chief of staff). You will be leaving the division. I want you to come up to Washington in two days. I will tell you then what this is all about. See you then." As I hung up the phone, my mind was racing with questions. I went to the commanding general's office and told him what General Meyer had said. He too was surprised and we attempted to figure out what this might be all about. We were not successful. If you recall in my introduction, I indicated significant decisions and milestones in my life which were not of my making. They came, in fact, from the greatest Friend anyone could have and that, of course, is Jesus Christ, the Son of God the Father.

CHAPTER 9

THE BEGINNING AND MORE A NEW COMMAND

General Meloy told me to take the next two days off so I could go to Washington. Later that day, I told the family about the phone call and my pending trip to Washington. I was deluged with questions about if we must move, where we might have to go, when we must move. In addition, the real question was, "Why?" Tom and Peg were again concerned if they had to change schools. Tom already had his class ring from the wrong school.

I contacted the joint staff and coordinated my visit to the Pentagon. I was to meet with the Chairman of the Joint Chiefs of Staff and the Secretary of Defense. Then I was to be briefed on some background information concerning possible missions. I proceeded to Washington and went directly to the Pentagon and to General Meyer's office. His office informed me that a briefing had been prepared for me and I was escorted to another office where I found at least 20 personnel in an office with a single desk and room for maybe 10 people. Before I could meet the men, a briefer started showing viewgraphs and speaking of several alternative plans for the conduct of a rescue attempt to free the United States Embassy staff in Iran. Some may recall that the embassy staff had been taken hostage on 4 November 1979 when a group of Iranian students stormed the embassy taking more than 60 Americans hostage.

As the briefer proceeded describing alternative courses of action, I interrupted him by stating loudly so everyone could hear me, "I am not certain as to why I am being given this classified information." There was a period of dead silence until one of the men said they were told to brief me on the various alternative plans the staff had considered so I would have a basis from which to start my planning for the mission. When I questioned why I would be doing such planning, there was another period of complete silence. Finally, one of the men asked, "Has the secretary of defense or the chairman not made it clear as to the formation of a new command?" Apparently, it was my priority mission. I responded that I was not scheduled to see those gentlemen until tomorrow. There was a gasp from the crowded room and the briefer said they had been told I would meet with the SECDEF before I received this briefing. I told them to proceed with the briefing and, if after my meeting with the SECDEF I had questions concerning the points raised in the briefing, I would contact them.

The next day, I met with the chairman of the Joint Chiefs of Staff and the Secretary of Defense. I was told I was to form a new highly classified joint command with, as its first and priority mission, freeing the American hostages in Iran. When I left this meeting, I went immediately to the Army staff. There I learned that they were already working with the other services for manning the new joint command. As I studied the proposed staffing and force structure of the new command, I questioned where this new command would be stationed. Some staff officers indicated the command should be stationed near the Washington, DC area, so guidance from the services and the joint staff could be rapidly passed. From previous experience, I knew that anytime a military unit had the joint staff or the services so close, they could browbeat the unit into doing things as they say is "not a good solution." I countered with the thought that the command should be retained at Fort Bragg where it would draw less attention from outsiders as well as providing some cushion for the command. I also questioned the required date for the command to be prepared for the rescue attempt. The desired date was the end of October, which ironically, was just before the November elections for president. This October date provided very little time to form and equip the command, to gain adequate and correct intelligence as to the location of every American being held, and to develop and rehearse an effective course of action.

When I returned to Fort Bragg, I informed the CG of the results of my trip. He was very interested and told me that I should leave the division so I could concentrate all efforts on developing the new command. He also released my aide so he could go with me. I knew an immediate need was for an office with a secure phone but, since the command was not officially formed yet, there was no office or phone. I knew that one unit on Fort Bragg would become a subordinate element of the new command, but I was not aware if the commander of the unit had been informed of the formation of the new command. I went to Colonel Beckwith, the Delta commander, and explained the situation. He gave me an office within his compound from which to work until the command was completely formed and could locate adequate office facilities. This was a temporary solution while we searched for a permanent location for our new headquarters.

From that office, I interviewed every officer and non-commissioned officer that arrived for assignment to the new command. It took several weeks for the entire 85+ members of the staff to arrive. In the interim, I searched for a temporary location for the command until new facilities could be constructed. I also wrestled with an unclassified name for the command. The commander of the post indicated we could have three World War II barracks that were usually occupied by the summer ROTC program. We had a large metal fence placed around the buildings and gradually moved into our temporary headquarters. We also gave the command a new name as the Joint Special Operations Command (JSOC).

While we continued to occupy the WWII barracks buildings, we wrestled with two significant problems. The first was to decide on the best of the courses of action identified at my earlier briefing at the Pentagon. We studied the after-action reports from the failed rescue attempt and isolated those activities from that attempt that needed correction. I felt it critical that we employ forces and equipment from within the command. I did not want to employ helicopters or personnel from outside the command. We listed a myriad of training and equipment requirements that would be continuously updated as we trained for the mission. We worked closely with the CIA and DIA to emphasize the need for current up-to-the-minute intelligence.

Another problem concerned a location for a new headquarters where proper coordination could be conducted along with the need for secure telephones and other equipment. We identified a large section of land that was Pope AFB property, but was butted up against Fort Bragg property. It offered the advantage of additional security because entrance to the property required passing through the gates of Pope AFB that were always manned by Air Force security personnel. On my next trip to Washington, I went to the undersecretary of defense to request priority funding for the new headquarters. I gave him a sketch of how the large two-story building should be designed to house the staff functions, large conference rooms, an operations center, a communications center, and much more. What I failed to think of, or mention, was windows. As a result, we ultimately ended up with a new headquarters building without a single window. Fortunately, this error helped with security concerns. In addition to the headquarters building, we requested construction of a building to contain a very large shredding machine to handle a vast number of classified documents and machines. We later provided the exact measurements of the enormous shredding machine that could demolish computers and anything metal or paper.

Photo #15: JSOC patch 1980

Over the next several weeks, the staff worked on courses of action for our mission, and we gathered mission essential equipment. One piece of equipment that was significant back in the 80's was our man-portable satellite radios. These radios were truly state of the art. During one of many demonstrations for distinguished visitors, we showed the chairman of the Joint Chiefs of Staff how we could send a message around the world. We had prepositioned two-man communications teams in Hawaii, on an island in the Indian Ocean, in Germany, and in the Pentagon. All these elements were equipped with the man-portable satellite radios. We asked the general to send a brief message to his secretary in the Pentagon. Then this message was transmitted over the satellite radio to the forward deployed teams. The message went around the world through the radios with the forward deployed teams to the radio at the general's office in the Pentagon. The chairman was so impressed that he directed his staff to procure the radios for his office and each of the unified commands.

Commanding this new organization brought with it many challenges. Establishing a secure and efficient working space for the staff was essential. We spent considerable time coordinating this effort while simultaneously learning the capabilities and limitations of each of the subordinate commands. Selecting the best course of action required testing and evaluating every aspect of each course of action through detailed rehearsals. The Carter administration still wanted a rescue before the November election. I argued that we should not attempt a rescue if we were not certain of the location of all hostages. If we pulled off a rescue but left several hostages behind, the mission could not be called a success. I also failed to believe a political reason for an execution date for conducting any mission of such magnitude was an insult to the troops undertaking the mission. The intelligence community was diligently working to locate every hostage, but this caused many delays. When we thought we had a lock on the hostage locations, we decided the best course of action and were in the middle of the rehearsal when President Reagan was being sworn in. It was then that Iran announced the release of the hostages. Our mission was overtaken by events. We were so very fortunate that the mission was scrubbed because subsequent intelligence gathered from the people held hostage showed that some of them were not located where our intelligence indicated they would be. I like to think the good Lord played a critical role in the scrubbing of the mission so that we could avoid a potentially disastrous failure.

With the American hostage mission no longer a requirement, we began working with other government agencies on potential missions in their area of interest. In addition, we studied and tested potential scenarios to include terrorists seizing luxury liners on the high seas, or possibly attempting to seize nuclear material being transported in the United States, or attacks against Olympic athletes during the Olympics to be conducted in California in 1984. All these efforts were closely coordinated with government agencies and the services so we could cooperate while simultaneously showing the capabilities of the command.

During one of the several capabilities demonstrations for key government and military personnel, I was approached by the director of the FBI, William H. Webster, with a request to meet with him and key FBI personnel in their Washington, DC offices in three weeks. I agreed and proceeded to the FBI Washington Offices on an established date and time. There were several FBI personnel at the meeting and, after introductions, Judge Webster asked me if JSOC would be willing to train a soon-to-be established counter-terrorist organization within the FBI. The judge then introduced me to Danny Coulson who had been designated as the commander of what we now know as the FBI Hostage Rescue Team (HRT). I agreed to develop a training program with Mr. Coulson. Upon my return to Fort Bragg, I informed the Delta Commander of the requirement and a training program was designed and developed. After several weeks of close coordination, the training program was implemented and I am proud of the portion JSOC played in the development of this significant FBI capability.

In January 1981, the Joint Chiefs of Staff ordered JSOC to devise a rescue operation for American prisoners of war being held in prison camps in Laos. Vice Admiral Jerry Tuttle came to Fort Bragg and briefed us on the information that the Defense Intelligence Agency (DIA) had concerning the possibility of Americans being held in Laos. He also arranged to have a tabletop-size model of the Laotian camp built based on satellite photos and delivered it to JSOC to help with the planning. We started initial planning in the event further clarification might determine a mission for JSOC. Subsequently, it was decided that a reconnaissance patrol should be sent to the target to get photography of any prisoners. When I was informed of the possibility of such a patrol, I insisted that Delta personnel conduct the reconnaissance. I wanted American eyes that I trusted to do the mission. The Central Intelligence Agency was adamant that they would use Thailand and Laos personnel, which they personally selected.

They did specify that one American from CIA would be included and I was unsuccessful in my argument when National Security Advisors (NSA) sided with the CIA. I believe the NSA later regretted that decision because the CIA's reconnaissance team performed so poorly. No Americans were included. The team was led by a former Royal Laotian Air Force pilot with no commando or special operations experience. The patrol used antiquated radios and equipment. The team needed climbing equipment so, apparently, some agency staff members went to a mountaineering shop and purchased white rope. JSOC heard about the problem and surreptitiously sent them olive-green rope that would not be easily spotted in the jungle. Photos taken were not clear enough to ascertain if the target was American. The potential mission was scrubbed when there was no proof of Americans being held at the Pham Louang camp.

This experience proved that JSOC must maintain a very close relationships with the national intelligence communities to include

CIA, DIA and NSA. An incident with the CIA indicated a potential break in the relationship. The agency staff contacted me with information that JSOC had released security information and as a result would no longer receive any intelligence from the agency. I immediately met with our intelligence personnel as well as those from our subordinate commands and verified that no such release had occurred. Subsequently I was to attend a meeting in Washington concerning the terrorism threat and in attendance at that meeting was the Director of the CIA, William Casey. While everyone was milling around in the meeting hall before the scheduled start time, I saw Mr. Casey seated at one of the head tables. I immediately went to him, introduced myself, and then told him I was very disappointed in the decision to withhold intelligence from JSOC because of some inaccurate information his agency had obtained. As I spoke to Mr. Casey, I saw the CIA Operations Director and several other agency personnel moving to our location in a very hostile manner. Mr. Casey stopped them and instructed them to sit down with me to clear the air about any problems that exist between the agency and JSOC. I thanked Mr. Casey and went to another table to talk with the Director. I explained what I had learned from our intelligence personnel and that it appeared the so-called release of classified information was during a training session with the CIA, National Security Agency (NSA) and the Defense Intelligence Agency (DIA). The training session was designed to establish procedures in the event classified information was inadvertently passed to outside agencies. I asked the Director to talk with the agency personnel who took part in the training to verify my information. He seemed to have no knowledge of the training session but agreed he would check into it. The JSOC intelligence staff subsequently received information that the restrictions on the command had been released.

Another prisoner problem arose with the capture of BG Dozier by Red Brigade guerrillas. He was taken prisoner from his apartment in Verona, Italy on December 17, 1981 by four Red Brigade guerrillas masquerading as plumbers. This capture shook the Pentagon because Dozier was NATO's deputy chief of staff for land forces in Southern Europe. We sent several personnel to work with the Italian Armed Forces and to determine if JSOC forces could be of assistance. The JSOC personnel worked with the Italian police special operations unit. It was this unit led by Major Perna that ultimately conducted the raid on an apartment in the northern Italian city of Padua that freed BG Dozier.

We learned quickly that, as a new and unique command, we could expect many visitors. Most of these visitors were interested in the capabilities of the command, so this entailed demonstrations of equipment and personnel. One such visitor was Vice President Bush and his entourage of secret service and administrative personnel. When we briefed the advance party of the secret service about what the VP would be shown, they immediately balked at the VP being in a room where bullets would be fired at silhouettes in several directions. As a result, we had to delete that portion of the demonstration. While Vice President Bush was in our headquarters, he saw an artistic drawing we had hung on a hall wall. It was a drawing of an obviously irritated Uncle Sam with his shirt sleeves rolled up and a newspaper rolled up in his right hand with some words visible about the American Embassy staff being held prisoner in Iran. Printed across the drawing in bold letters was, "UNCLE SAM WANTS TO KICK ASS." The VP indicated President Reagan would love to have that drawing. During a subsequent visit to the White House, I gave one of the staff personnel the framed drawing for the President. Later, when we were still meeting with the staff, President Reagan entered the room with the drawing and said he wanted to thank me personally. He had a photographer with him, and he took several photos of the president and me with the drawing. One of those photos hangs proudly in my home office.

After three years in command, I was looking at probable reassignment when I received a request from the Army Forces

Photo #16: VP Bush visits JSOC 1981

Command (FORSCOM) to meet with the commander. I traveled to FORSCOM headquarters and reported to the four-star commanding officer. I had no idea what this meeting was about but learned, in a minute or two after reporting to him, that this was a proverbial a** chewing! Somehow, the Army leadership thought that, as commander of this special unit, I was bending too much to the other services and government agencies and disregarding my loyalty to the Army. I knew the Army staff did not appreciate my stand on the control of MFP-11 but I did not appreciate the degree of hostility. He went so far as to inform me that, when I leave command of this unit, I will not be given command of any Army division. Hearing that threat was the same as being told my career in the military was over. I departed that office and FORSCOM very upset and disgruntled, to say the least.

After I returned to the unit, I wondered if this attitude and evaluation of my performance by the FORSCOM commander was held by those superior officers for which I worked. On my weekly trip to Washington, I went to General Vessey, Chairman of the Joint Chiefs of Staff, another four-star general. This is, of course, the same General Vessey that I had served under at Fort Carson as his chief of staff. I told him of my visit to FORSCOM. He was somewhat shocked and irritated and told me to continue with the work I had been doing. I also spoke to the secretary of defense and his response was similar with no indication my performance was unsatisfactory. When I completed my trip and returned to the unit, my morale was considerably higher.

Another series of events, which took considerable time and effort for the staff and the units, were demonstrations of our capabilities. I recall one when we were asked to provide a demonstration for select personnel from the joint staff and the office of the SECDEF. As we prepared for the demonstration, we were visited by the four-star Air Force Chief of Staff. He wanted to know how we were demonstrating the Air Force aircraft. We informed him that, in the night portion of the demonstration, we would show total blackout landings by a C-130,

Photo #17: President Reagan 1983

a four-engine propeller-driven cargo aircraft (a real workhorse of an airplane), a C141, a 4-engine jet personnel and cargo aircraft, and a C5, the largest jet aircraft in the Air Force inventory. Total blackout means no visible lights on the runway and no lights on the aircraft. The general was a little nervous about trying a C5 landing with no lights and thought the pilot should illuminate the landing lights shortly before touchdown to verify the center of the runway and his height from the ground. I informed him all spectators would be wearing night vision goggles and, if the C5 turned on its landing lights, even momentarily, it would destroy the night vision of the spectators. The general gave an okay, but I know he was very nervous. For those who have never been in or have never seen a C5, it is the largest aircraft in the Air Force with the pilots' cockpit almost two stories off the ground and the rear cargo area capable of carrying six AH-64 Apache Long Bow Attack Helicopters, or fifteen HUMVEE trucks. Landing it while wearing night vision goggles would be a difficult task and they did it beautifully.

C H A P T E R   1 0

URGENT FURY CLOSE TO A COMPLETE FAILURE

The demonstration, day and night, went very well but, when we were flying back to Fort Bragg, General Vessey, the Chairman of the Joint Chiefs of Staff, pulled me aside and whispered that I should become very familiar with the island of Grenada in the Caribbean. The island of Grenada is one of the southernmost islands in the Lesser Antilles which make up the eastern boundary of the Caribbean Sea and the western boundary of the Atlantic Ocean. The next day, I directed the staff to ascertain everything they could about the island and brief me on their findings. Even before I could receive the briefing, we were alerted to conduct operations on the island with several specific objectives. The initial command and control for the operation was to be directly from the chairman of the Joint Chiefs of Staff to my command. We were given minimum time to develop our course of action for the operation. We elected to use C5 aircraft to deliver two assault forces and UH-60 Blackhawk helicopters to the island of Barbados in the Caribbean. This force would assemble the UH-60's and fly to Grenada and secure 3 objectives while the main force would fly from Pope AFB adjacent to Ft. Bragg in C-130 aircraft. One

Photo #18: Captured Anti-Aircraft weapon Grenada 1983

Ranger company, in three C-130's, would conduct a parachute assault to seize and clear the airfield. The remainder of the Ranger battalion would then air-land on the cleared runway and move to secure the airfield and the True-Blue Campus where the American students were located. The True-Blue Campus was a housing and school area which was a relatively short distance from the airfield. The forces were developing their internal plan for their missions when we received new guidance. Because this operation was taking place in the Caribbean, it was directed that it would be under the control of the Commander and Chief of the Atlantic (CINCLANT). We were directed to brief CINCLANT on our planned course of action.

Within a day, we had prepared our briefing and flew to Norfolk. The briefing went well, but the CINCLANT staff had little or no knowledge of our forces or their capabilities. As a result, they immediately questioned why we insisted on an H-hour of 0230. We explained the advantage of night operations; however, they were reluctant to accept our explanation and rationale. They questioned our ability to land helicopters and C-130 aircraft without appropriate lighting. We raised the issue about maps because, in coordinating with the United States Mapping Agency, we were having difficulty obtaining military maps of the island. We ended this meeting with considerable guidance and confusion and an indication that CINCLANT was thinking of having another command placed between CINCLANT and my headquarters. We were rapidly approaching the established D-day for this operation when two significant events impacted on everything we had planned. Just days before we were to implement our plans, the Marine barracks in Lebanon were destroyed by truck bombs killing 220 Marines. That same afternoon, I briefed the chairman, the service chiefs, and their operational deputies in the Pentagon on our plans. The briefing was proceeding very well when the commandant of the Marine Corp interrupted and said that the Marines had to be included in the operation because of the bombing in Lebanon. After considerable discussion, the chairman decided the Marines would conduct an amphibious landing on part of the island and we should coordinate our actions. With this decision, CINCLANT established a three-star headquarters to provide command and control of the Marines and my force.

Unfortunately, this new commander and his staff had no idea as to what JSOC was or anything about the capabilities of the JSOC units. The Marines also had no knowledge of JSOC, the uniforms we wore, or the assault techniques our forces used. This headquarters was allegedly contacted by the Marine units conducting the operation to argue that they could not conduct the operation under cover of darkness; hence, a new H-hour of 0630 was ordered. This would mean parachute assault and helicopter assault all during daylight hours. With this change of H-hour came orders to brief CINCLANT on all the changes. This briefing was to be given on D-Day minus 1, the day before we were to launch the operation.

This new briefing at CINCLANT was attended by several new players. The commanding general of the 82nd Airborne Division was present as well as several state department representatives. The operation was now named "Urgent Fury." We provided our briefing as we had in the past, but the state department representative continued to interrupt. On one occasion, he informed us that three state department personnel must join whatever forces would have the mission to secure and protect the Governor General of Grenada. When I asked if these people were trained at fast roping from a helicopter, his only reply was that we would have to land for them to exit the chopper. At the next interruption, the state department representative said it was essential that the prison be included as an initial objective. When I asked why it had to be seized, he indicated several people are probably being held as political prisoners. When I asked who these people might be, he said they did not know. I asked why it is an essential initial target, and he said it was to protect any political prisoners. I wanted to say, "That was one stupid response," but I held my tongue. The admiral concurred with the state department, so the prison was added as an essential objective to be taken at H-hour. Of course, this meant change of missions for critical forces which were scheduled to launch in less than 18 hours. Delta had done all their planning to land adjacent to the True-Blue campus and to secure the students, and now their objective was changed to secure the prison. The rangers who were to secure the airfield now had the added mission of securing the students. As many of us have learned over these numerous years, last minute changes to complex events lead to disaster. In this case, trying to seize all objectives in broad daylight and having objectives you cannot properly control led to several helicopters damaged by enemy fire. One Blackhawk helicopter was shot down with the pilot killed. Several passengers were wounded and several Rangers wounded or killed.

I left the briefing very upset. As usual, staff officers who never served in an outfit like JSOC were making decisions that made the job of the JSOC forces much more difficult and dangerous. Upon my return to Fort Bragg, I found everyone deeply engrossed in preparations for departure. When I briefed the Delta commanders on the need to seize the prison, there were many questions as to how to determine good guys from bad guys. The only solution was to take over the prison and continue to hold all existing prisoners until additional clarification was made available: not a very good solution, especially when we later learned that there were no political prisoners. The Ranger commander also had to make major last-minute changes to seize the airfield and to secure the students. If that sounds relatively simple, just know that it is not.

When we were satisfied that everything was moving, we loaded the C-130 command and control aircraft and took off. Within this command and control aircraft, we had communications to each of the subordinate commanders, our higher headquarters (the three-star discussed earlier), and to each of the airframes taking part in the operation. From Fort Bragg to the island of Grenada is 1,940 miles, so we had a long flight ahead of us. As the lead element of one Ranger company loaded in three C-130 aircraft was approaching the island of Grenada, my deputy commander, an Air Force brigadier general, informed me that the lead aircraft had lost its inertial navigation system (INS) so could not be certain of its approach to the island. I was concerned about losing the runway clearance company and asked if the number 1 bird that had lost its INS could fly on the wing of number 2 in the formation, and jump when the lead aircraft started jumping. The answer was that they were in a storm and could not even see the other planes. I immediately radioed the Ranger Battalion commander and told him to prepare another company for clearing the runway. This meant the new company had to put on parachutes and drop on the objective as soon as possible. That also sounds routine, but putting a parachute on when you are on the ground is difficult enough. Putting it on in a plane when you have a weapon with live ammunition that must be strapped to you is a tough job in a very little space. You certainly cannot afford one mistake because it could mean your chute will not open properly or may not even open. While all this is going on, the commander and his lieutenants would also have to be given new mission guidance which had to be given to each soldier. Remember, talking in a C-130 is extremely difficult because of the noise.

While we worked to solve the Ranger problem, our other strike forces were in route from the island of Barbados on Blackhawk helicopters. The Delta forces were headed for the prison while Seal Team 6 troops were headed for the radio station and the governor general's mansion. As soon as we received the word that the runway was cleared, we commenced air landing the remaining Rangers. As this was progressing, Delta was attempting to secure the prison, and Seal Team 6 the governor's mansion. The prison excursion did not go well. The hillside adjacent to the prison was crowded with anti-aircraft weapons and one Blackhawk was quickly shot down. The remaining Blackhawks were taking fire while discharging the Delta force yet were able to evacuate the area and land adjacent to the airfield. All the Blackhawks were riddled with bullet holes. One of those men seriously wounded was Major Jerry Boykin, a Delta Squadron Commander. He was struck in the shoulder by an explosive 40mm shell. Had the state department representative not forced the seizure of the prison as a priority mission, we could have avoided many wounded and damage to our helicopter fleet. We never did determine if there were political prisoners in the prison.

Operations at the governor's mansion were moving slowly. Members of Seal Team 6 had fast roped from their helicopters and entered the mansion. They had secured the governor general and were providing him security. Cuban fighters were close to the mansion and were taking Seal Team 6 under fire. The Seal

Team 6 element that was responsible for taking control of the radio station was also in a firefight. Meanwhile, the Rangers were making considerable headway on securing the True-Blue Campus and the students. For those not familiar with this school, a considerable number of United States students attend it to attain a medical doctorate degree. As the seizure of True-Blue campus was being accomplished, some of the Rangers had travelled in gun-jeeps to a point where they came under fire by the Cubans. Several of the Rangers were wounded or killed. Seizure of the Radio Station was still in contention as the Cubans continued their efforts to retake the station. The Seal Team 6 element had fought off the first attempt by the Cubans, but it was apparent, with the small number of Seals in this element, that they would not be so fortunate if another attack were to come. The leader destroyed the radio equipment, evacuated the sight, and moved to the ocean a short distance away. There they swam out several hundred yards and were picked up by a destroyer. Meanwhile, my command and control bird landed on the island and we moved to a large airfield building under construction where we established our command post.

As we consolidated our forces, we were informed the 82nd Airborne Brigade would be landing shortly. I received a radio call from the commanding general of the 82nd and was asked if the runway was clear or if they should para-drop the entire brigade. I recommended air landing in view of the narrow width of the runway, and a jump altitude of 500 feet was the only way to avoid troopers drifting into the ocean. He finally agreed and air-landed. When the commander of the 82nd arrived, I went to him and informed him of what my command had secured. I also informed him that I would extricate all my forces so we could avoid friendly fire problems. He insisted the Rangers remain. I pointed out to him that they had been operating for over 30+ hours with no sleep. He still insisted and finally got the 3-star admiral to agree with him.

As we evacuated those students that desired to depart the island, I turned control of the island over to the commander of the 82nd. We had landed a C-141 rigged for evacuation of wounded personnel. When all our forces (minus the Rangers) were evacuated, I boarded the medevac C-141 and we departed Grenada in route to Puerto Rico. Prior to the commencement of the operation, we had alerted the hospital in Puerto Rico that wounded personnel would be transported to their site for treatment. Initially, we headed to the island of Puerto Rico. While in route, I verified that most of the wounded were from Fort Bragg, NC, or Fort Jackson, SC. I had an opportunity to speak to Jerry Boykin, a squadron commander of Delta. He was in considerable pain with his shoulder ripped apart by the exploding 40mm shell. I contacted the XVIII Airborne Corps Commander at Fort Bragg and asked if the hospital at Fort Bragg could handle the influx of wounded personnel. When he verified that the hospital at Fort Bragg could handle the wounded, we changed our flight. Walking among the wounded and talking to many, they were thrilled we were headed to Fort Bragg instead of Puerto Rico.

Urgent Fury came so very close to being a complete disaster. I thank the good Lord, to this day, for the results we were able to gain. As an outcome of the many problems encountered, one would think that CINCLANT would have scheduled a hot wash or after-action review of every aspect of the mission with every player present so we could learn from our mistakes. There was no hot wash by CINCLANT or by the joint staff in the Pentagon. As Noel Koch, Deputy Assistant Secretary of Defense for Africa, and Director of Special Planning with responsibility for anti-terrorism and counterterrorism, as well as the restoration of special operations forces during the Reagan administration, wrote in his book, *Operation Urgent Fury: The Invasion of Grenada*, 1983:

"Following every American military undertaking, be it an exercise to hone skills or an operation to put them to use, the undertaking is closely reviewed and evaluated to extract the lessons to be learned.

It begins with what is called a "hot scrub" or "hot wash" aimed at extracting information while events are fresh in the minds of the participants. General Scholtes remembers asking repeatedly when the "hot wash" on Urgent Fury was to be scheduled. "Soon, soon, we're getting to it," he was assured. There was no hot wash."

Based on what we in JSOC learned, we too planned for a detailed review of all events by all our forces. As a first step, we asked the commanders to do their reviews and then we planned a full-scale hot-wash after checking with CINCLANT and DOD for all their input. Unfortunately, we never received input from those headquarters. As a result, I foresaw similar problems in the future when major commands were not aware of our organization, mission, and capabilities. One of our key considerations for all missions was to rehearse every detail in the conference room and in the field environment. Because of continued changes of the overall concept of operations by CINCLANT and the department of state, there was no time for rehearsals for Urgent Fury. Urgent Fury should have awakened some of the leadership in the military and the government to include Congress and the Executive Branch but, as we investigated another significant event such as invasion of Iraq, or the invasion of Afghanistan with no apparent plan for ending the conflict, we see that most were still asleep.

A few months later, at a meeting at the West Wing of the White House, the subject of the 1984 Olympics at Los Angeles came up. We were told that the president wanted JSOC at Los Angeles in the event of a terrorist incident. I explained to the White House staff that we did not think it would be a wise move for us to be at Los Angeles because, under the law "Posse Comitatus," Federal Forces could not be engaged in police type activities. JSOC could not arrest anyone or perform any other police functions. I was told to have JSOC at the Olympics, but to take no action unless ordered by the president. We did deploy our forces, yet maintained total control of all activities so that our presence would not be known. When we first deployed, we did not take our military helicopter assets, but we quickly learned that driving on the California highways was difficult at best. We subsequently rented civilian helicopters. Thankfully, we made it through the Olympics without any deployment or counter terrorist activities. Someone did steal a large gasoline tanker truck that we thought might be used by a terrorist, but the police found the tanker and the thief. He had thought he could sell the gasoline.

CHAPTER 11

FROM JSOC TO THE 2ND ARMORED DIVISION

In 1984, I received orders to assume command of the 2nd Armored Division at Fort Hood, Texas. As I read the orders, I had to smile as I recalled the words of the FORSCOM commander that I would "never command an Army Division." I must admit that my tour as the Commander of JSOC was the highlight of my military career so, as I left Fort Bragg, there was a feeling of regret. Simultaneously, I was very appreciative of the fact that the Army would allow me to command a division.

The move to Texas from Fort Bragg was a new experience for the family because our daughter, Peg, was now 17 years old and the proud owner of a horse named Keelo. Peg had taken up competitive riding at Fort Bragg. She loved her horse and was a talented equestrian. Keelo was in his trailer behind our car for the long and much slower trip. We had to arrange for and reserve horse stables for every stop. Planning the trip kept my secretary very busy, but it worked like clockwork. Arriving at Fort Hood and moving into our house went smoothly. Meetings with the corps commander and his staff went well. Ironically, some of the meetings with the officers of the division did not go as smoothly. The fact that I was an infantryman about to assume command of an armored division stuck in the craw of many armored officers or, as infantrymen call them, "Tread Heads." Then, coupling that with the fact that my assignment for the past four years was with Special Operations, which has no correlation to armored operations, caused further consternation.

The change of command ceremony was not as good as I expected. The culprit was the one unit I would never have expected and that was the division band. The band looked pathetic in their marching and I immediately questioned why a band as large as ours had only two tubas on the rear row. I made a very harsh decision and relieved the bandmaster. After considering the situation in greater detail, I told my aide to have the band assembled informally outside of their barracks area. I went to the site and explained why I had taken the action and why I was disappointed with the band's performance at the change of command. Then I informed the band that I was wrong in relieving the band master without first determining precisely why the band appeared as it did. Then and there, I reinstated the bandmaster and told him that, if it was funds, personnel, or time, I wanted to know exactly what the band needed to be the best division band in our Army. Within six months, we had a band of which everyone could be proud.

Following the change of command ceremonies, I waited until the following day to have an officer's call where I could speak to all the officers. We met at the post theater where I told them that I did not intend to make changes for the sake of changes, that they were to continue training as usual until they heard new guidance. I also informed them my office would publish a schedule of briefings from each major command. The briefings were to discuss their concerns as to the training and their recommendations for changes in training procedures.

The first month made it clear to me that we were placing too much emphasis on being "night fighters" to the detriment of other training. I had observed numerous night operations and found that coordination and cooperation between the armored and infantry forces was lacking. I knew that, in almost every possible conflict, we could anticipate the division as part of a larger force and not operating alone under its own command. In most situations, there would be other infantry and armor divisions so control would rest at the corps level. As a result, single division night operations would seldom be the norm. I was interested in a force that could fight equally as well in day and night. I issued orders to better balance the day and night training scenarios.

As we balanced the day and night operations, the division headquarters were preparing for a move they had anticipated over a year. A new headquarters building had been under construction and was close to being made available. The headquarters had been operating out of WWII buildings. They needed considerable repair and kept the staff separated physically causing coordination to be hampered. The move into the new building brought a smile to so many faces. The proximity of all staffs in one building greatly added to staff efficiency.

As my first year in command came to an end, I envisioned a training exercise for the division that would test our ability to move rapidly while proving the ability of the support command and other support elements to provide necessary logistical support. I laid out what I referred to as "HOW 1." The division's nickname from World War II was "Hell on Wheels" and I thought this dynamic exercise should be "Hell on Wheels 1" shortened to HOW 1. The staff worked diligently on preparing a briefing for the command and the III Corps Headquarters, which was also located on Fort Hood. I wanted the corps to know what we planned because it was going to be costly in terms of spare parts and fuel consumption. The plan was to have the maneuver brigades move a minimum of 10 miles each day as one might expect in an offense in Europe. They did not just drive around for the 10 miles. Ranges were designated along routes for every weapon in the brigade. How the brigades moved was up to the commander, but they must move. The real test was on the division support command (DISCOM). They had to deliver supplies and fuel to the brigades over a long distance to determine what problems we could anticipate for the command. The exercise did not go without problems, but we learned a great deal about the difficulty of providing support to a fast-moving mechanized force. HOW 1 was a tough but useful exercise for the division.

Another exercise drew attention and provided something for the people of the surrounding communities to witness. This was a live fire demonstration that coupled my division with our local National Guard Brigade. We set up bleachers for over a thousand people and a thousand more were seated on the ground. So many people arrived that we had to delay the start to allow them to park and walk the distance to the stands. They witnessed tanks and Bradley Infantry Fighting vehicles firing on the move, and artillery of all types to include medium range missiles firing into the impact area and the devastation they caused. To me, and to so many with whom I spoke, the demonstration was a complete success. To some of the staff officers from Forces Command, it was too costly.

As I entered the second year in command, I had a series of visitors from the United States Senate. These were staffers for Senator Cohen and two other senators. They wanted to talk about some potential problems concerning Special Operations in the military. Apparently, the subject of military special operations forces was being considered by the House and Senate. The House of Representatives were considering placement of military Special Operations forces under the CIA. The 3 services, Army, Navy and Air Force, were opposed to any changes, but especially changes in the control of MFP-11 funds which were those provided for Special Operations Forces and their equipment. Senator Cohen and several other members of the Senate wanted me to come before the Senate Armed Services Committee (SASC) and explain some of the problems with current command

and control arrangements. I had told the staffers previously that I saw the need for centralized control of Special Operations Forces and the Major Funding Program (MFP-11). Presently, all MFP-11 funds are controlled by the services and they are the first area of cuts when a reduction is ordered. The greatest roadblock to any changes of existing policy was the services. The Army, Navy, and Air Force wanted complete control of their forces and, more importantly, the funding for Special Operations. As Commander of JSOC, I argued continuously that MFP-11 funds must be controlled by the commander of the Special Operations Forces. As a 2-star versus several 4-star general, I always lost that argument. I argued also that the training and doctrine for special operations forces must be centralized. At that point, the senators wanted me to go before the SASC and spell out my rationale. They emphasized that the military could expect major changes in organization and structure as well as command and control based on the feeling in Washington that changes must be made. I told the staffers that I did not want to go before the Senate in uniform or while I was in service because I knew I would be going directly against the wishes of the Army. I put a hold on any briefings before Congress.

While in command of the division, we had many visitors. One visit almost cost my life, but, once again, it showed the good Lord stood by my side. We had visiting German generals who desired to see our Abrams tanks in action, so I was to meet them at our tank gunnery range. My headquarters helipad was directly behind our headquarters building and my aide and I walked to the waiting helicopter and boarded in our usual way. As the pilot lifted off and started to gain altitude, everything was going smoothly. Suddenly, at about 200-300 feet from the ground, there was a very large sound like an explosion. It was a blown engine. The pilots immediately searched for a possible landing site. He was concerned about trying to land back on the command headquarters pad because of the proximity of the buildings. He was having considerable problems controlling the chopper with no engine.

There were no other landing pads in our immediate area. The pilots headed the limping chopper toward a helipad some distance away. Unfortunately, the autorotation and the rate of fall all ran out before we could reach the pad. We crashed with tremendous force. I do not recall anything about the crash, I only know what I had been told by witnesses. Apparently, the outboard facing seat that I was in broke loose and sent my head breaking through the clear plastic portion of the roof of the chopper.

My aide was sitting on the rear bench and suffered a broken leg, while both pilots suffered leg and head injuries. I have no recollection how we got out of the bird or where I was. At the same time of the accident, JoAnn was hosting the German generals' wives and they were shopping in Southern Pines several miles from Fort Bragg. When she was informed of the accident, she was immediately transported to the Fort Hood hospital. When she first saw me, she thought I was dead. Ambulances had transported all the injured to the Fort Hood hospital. After numerous tests and scans, I was transported to a hospital in Waco, Texas that specialized in head injuries. Several days later, I was being transported in a wheelchair down the hall of the Waco hospital when I regained my senses and asked the medic where I was. He quickly rolled me into a doctor's office where I learned that I had been in the hospital over a week and had entered the hospital with a very large blood clot on my brain. The doctor ordered an immediate scan of the head and, when the scan was delivered to him, he called several doctors into his office to view it. They all were astounded because the blood clot had disappeared. The doctors had no explanation as to how the clot could have disappeared. I will always believe that my Lord Jesus performed another miracle on my behalf.

Since the doctors were unable to say how the blood clot had disappeared, the Corps Commander, General Saint, ordered me to stay away from the division for 30 days and to rest and undergo additional testing. To me, this was like a 30-day death sentence. I was naturally concerned about the division and training objectives that

I wanted accomplished in the next month. I also wondered what I would do while restricted to the house except for medical treatment for a full month. Someone suggested I purchase a computer so I bought an Apple 2E. I bet some of you reading this had never heard of such an Apple computer. Remember, that was 35 years ago (at the time of this writing, it is 2019). The computer was not up to the par of those of today, but I learned a great deal about computers and Apple software. I was still about to go stir crazy when the 30 days finally ended.

Sometime later, as my two years with the division were about to end, I attended a meeting with the other division commanders in Washington D.C. During that meeting, General Wickam, the Army Chief of Staff, informed me that he had selected me to be the Chief of Staff of 8th Army in Korea where I could gain my third star. Under any circumstance, I would have jumped at this assignment, but something held me back. When I replied to General Wickam, it was as if I was not talking. I said something like, "I appreciate the assignment sir, but I just cannot go to Korea at this time. My daughter just graduated high school and now would not be a good time to leave her. I will submit my retirement papers as soon as possible." My good Lord knew, of course, that this meant my departing the Army after 35 years.

CHAPTER 12

BEGINNING OF CIVILIAN LIFE

The next few weeks were preparing for the change of command of the division, determining where the family should move, and what activity I should undertake. I did not want anything to do with the many corporations that take advantage of our Defense Department. When one spends many years in the service of our country, they learn there are two major groups that impact our military the most. First is the Congress of the United States. Many years ago, Congress consisted of many men that had served our nation in the armed forces. Today, we have very few members of Congress who know anything about the military. There are only a few exceptions in the form of newcomers that have served in Afghanistan, Iraq, and Syria. I pray that somehow the older members, who have done little in their lives except be members of Congress, will listen to these military veterans. Military ware corporations are another group which I wanted to stay away from. They charge excessively for their products. When I commanded JSOC, lobbyists from one of these corporations convinced members of Congress to buy two patrol boats for JSOC. The last thing JSOC needed was patrol boats. It took a lot of talking and time wasted to turn off that one.

I wanted to stay away from anything to do with Department of Defense so no one could say my decision to leave the service was to benefit myself with a well-paying government job. I figured 2 or 3 years and then look at my options. I did recall the concerns of the Senate about Special Operations, but I was not ready to talk to them. I finally elected to join a friend in the lumber business. Wickes Lumber was originally in the northern states and was spreading into the southern states. I started with some schooling at a lumberyard in Austin, Texas and, during that time, rented a home in Austin. After about two months, the president of Wickes asked if I would move to Atlanta, Georgia for additional training. They were willing to move the family and our possessions, so off we went to Atlanta. We purchased a home in a suburb of Atlanta and I went daily to learn the lumberyard trade. After a month or two, I was given a lumberyard and store in Tucker, another suburb of Atlanta.

Shortly thereafter, I received another call from the Senate staffers. They were increasingly concerned about the probability of major and sweeping changes in the future of Special Operations and felt a congressional bill would be passed. Again, they asked me to reconsider going before the SASC. I informed them I was ready, so we agreed on a time and date. On the agreed date, I flew to Washington, went to the Pentagon, and waited for the appropriate time to take a cab over to the Capitol. When I arrived, I was escorted to the SASC. There I briefed the SASC and answered many questions. When I left, I felt uneasy. I was concerned that I had not gotten my points across. I was transported back to the General Officer Management office (GOMO) in the Pentagon and, as soon as I arrived, I was informed that Senate staffers had called and asked if I would return to the Senate. I returned the call and then went right back to the Capitol. I was escorted to a room with numerous senators. Senator Cohen asked if I would cover with these senators many of the points I had made to the SASC. I spent over two hours talking and answering questions. There was unanimity that the House plan to place all military special operations under the CIA was not feasible. They agreed with my recommendation that a 4-star command equal to each of the Unified Commands had to be established, which would control the training, doctrine, and operations of all special operations forces and would control all MFP-11 funds. In April 1987, the United States Special Operations Command (USSOCOM), with General Jim Lindsey as the commanding general, was activated at MacDill Air Force Base in Florida. The command has control of all MFP-11 funds. The Goldwater-Nichols Act that resolved the Special Operations problems also made significant changes within the entire defense structure of the United States.

After my ordeal in Washington, I continued with Wickes Lumber for two years. I decided then that I had stayed away from the Department of Defense long enough. I accepted an offer that interested me the most and that was as a consultant to Analytic Services (ANSER). This not-for-profit company located in Virginia was contracted with USSOCOM to do their mission analysis. I was initially brought on as a consultant and flew from Atlanta to Washington every Monday and returned to Atlanta on Friday. When ANSER decided to open an office in Tampa, Florida a short distance from MacDill AFB, they asked me to work full-time. I wanted to accept the offer but hesitated because it meant selling the house in a lousy housing market and finding a home in the Tampa vicinity. After much thought and many prayers, JoAnn and I decided it was a good move and offer. I moved to Tampa and rented an apartment while JoAnn remained near Atlanta at Lithonia, Georgia and worked with a realtor trying to sell the house. After a year, we decided JoAnn would come to Tampa and turn the house over to the realtor. We lived in apartments for the next few years and finally sold the house in Atlanta and purchased a home in Florida. I thanked the good Lord that the house in Atlanta had sold and that everything was going well with ANSER. I then went full-time with ANSER as the project manager. A year later, I was promoted to Vice President for Special Operations.

During the winter of 2000, I was having trouble with pain and, after several tests and scans, the doctors gave me the bad news that he thought I had pancreatic cancer. Surgery was necessary to verify the cancer and to take what actions were necessary. As most of us are aware, pancreatic cancer is deadly and most that are diagnosed with it die within six months. This was not the news we wanted or needed and scheduled a date for the surgery in June 2001. With this bad news, I elected to retire from ANSER. I knew that recuperating from the surgery would be extensive, so I would not be able to properly perform for the company.

The name of the surgery was "Whipple" and that seemed innocuous. When one looks at the description, it is not very pretty: *"The Whipple procedure, also officially known as pancreatic oduodenectomy, involves removal of the head (wide part) of the pancreas next to the first part of the small intestine (duodenum). It also involves removal of the duodenum, a portion of the common bile duct, gallbladder, and sometimes part of the stomach."* When the lengthy surgery was completed, the surgeon told JoAnn there was no cancer. We were certainly thrilled with that news but, just two weeks later while I was still on the mend from the surgery, my surgeon came to my room and notified me I should get a second opinion. I did not take that news very well and had trouble controlling myself when I asked what he was talking about: "A second opinion about what?" I wondered. He had already completed the surgery. When the nurses came in and tried to calm me down, they said I needed to go to Tampa General Hospital where the doctor that headed the pancreatic cancer board was located. Just three months after my first surgery, I met with that doctor who told me that, to truly test if a pancreas is cancerous, requires removal of a large piece and then an examination under microscopes of sections of that entire piece. The first surgeon did not cut off a section but did needle biopsy, which is not an effective procedure. When I asked what next, he said I had to undergo another operation and he would perform it. The second Whipple surgery was conducted and, thanks to our good Lord, the results were negative.

CHAPTER 13

MAJOR CHANGES IN MY PERSONAL LIFE

In 2001, I noted that JoAnn was showing the signs of dementia and, as a result, I elected to fully retire. JoAnn's dementia became full blown in 2002 when she daily tried to leave the house to walk down the street to her mother's house when, in fact, her mother never lived in Florida and had died several years prior. I took her to a neurologist and he indicated that, in his opinion, she was suffering with Alzheimer's. Over the next few years, her memory declined to the point she did not know she had children and could never be left alone. The neurologist and several of our friends advised me to commit her to a care facility. I hesitated in hopes that she would reverse the signs of memory loss. Every day was becoming more difficult because JoAnn would leave the house whenever she could sneak out. Neighbors would call and tell me they saw her walking down the street or on the golf course. I would have to drive or run to find her and return her home. There were other ugly signs that I would prefer not describing. To those who have not witnessed the terminal months of this disease, there is no way I can describe the full effects. I pray none of you will have to deal with a loved one with Alzheimer's.

On a happier note, in 2005 I received some very special recognition in the form of the "2005 Bull Simons Award." This award is presented annually to the individual selected for major contributions to the Special Operations community and is presented at a formal dinner gathering for the Special Operations forces. I was especially pleased that my two sons were able to attend and to watch over their mother while I received the award. When the citation for the award is read, the awardee is always proud of what he accomplished. But, did he really do it all alone? If we could look into Heaven and into God's trophy room, I imagine we would see thousands of duplicates of our trophies that were awarded to God for all He did concerning the same award that people felt they won on their own.

Finally, in 2007, I had to admit JoAnn to an assisted living facility in Florida. I was asked to stay away from the facility for 3 days for her to acclimate to the new environment. After the 3 days, I went to visit only to find someone had stolen her diamond wedding rings, her new shoes, and much of her clothing. I raised a big ruckus and the management claimed she flushed the ring and clothing down the toilet, and probably threw the shoes in the trash. When I asked why they were not observing her more closely, they merely frowned and said that is impossible. As a result, I searched for a better care facility. I came across what appeared to be the right facility called Homewood in Sun City Center, Florida. After talking to the manager and the nurses, I decided to transfer JoAnn to that facility. I was not pleased with the cost of $5,000 each month, but that was the going rate for facilities with high marks. The manager and a nurse from Homewood drove to the other facility, picked up JoAnn, and transported her to their facility. The Homewood facility was about 20 miles from the house making my visits twice a day too much. I placed the house in River Hills on the market and started preparing for a move to a new house located in Sun City Center, Florida.

One afternoon, during my visit with JoAnn, I noted that she was having difficulty breathing. When I informed one of the caregivers'

Photo #19: Bull Simon award 1995

staff, they immediately called one of the nurses. The nurse examined JoAnn and said she should be taken immediately to the hospital for a detailed examination. I said I would drive her to the hospital unless the nurse thought we needed an ambulance. She told me to go ahead and take her to the emergency room. We loaded JoAnn in the car and I drove her to the Brandon, Florida hospital emergency room. After a short wait, the doctor examined JoAnn and said it was pneumonia and she would be admitted to the hospital. It was two weeks later that she was released and I could return her to Sun City Center. Unfortunately, the Homewood facility had taken additional patients during JoAnn's absence, so they gave her a temporary room in a different facility. This facility was considered insecure for Alzheimer's' patients because the patients could reach outside doors that had no interior locks. They assigned two nurses to be with JoAnn at all times to include when she was asleep in her room. I was never told that the cost of her room and the nurse watch dogs would be $15,000.00 a month. When the first bill arrived, I was furious because every time I visited JoAnn during that month, the two nurses who were supposed to be taking care of her every need were watching TV in her room. On two visits, I found JoAnn lying in the bed filthy from a bowel movement. The room smelled, but the two nurses were still watching TV. I overreacted and grabbed the TV from the shelf and carried it to the main nurses' station with several expletives. I explained to the senior nurse on duty that these two nurses were not performing their duties appropriately. After the next bill of $15,000 I went to the senior manager and informed him I was removing JoAnn from his facilities unless he placed her immediately back at the Homewood facility that was equipped to care for Alzheimer patients. At that time, he gave orders to move her back, so I was at least thankful for that.

Meanwhile, I was still working to get the house in River Hills ready for the move to Sun City Center. I was trying to remove the boxes of Christmas decorations and many other boxes of stuff from the attic. I wasn't watching my step when some board gave way and I crashed through the ceiling of the garage. I was able to stop my fall, but only my elbows were keeping me from falling completely through the ceiling. I could not hold long and I fell to the very hard concrete floor. I lay on the floor stunned, but nothing was broken. I spent quite some time thanking my Holy Father. I slowly finished emptying the attic area with great caution and stiffness. I hired a handyman and he repaired the ceiling like new.

Fortunately, a buyer showed up and the River Hills home was no longer on the market. I made the necessary arrangements to move to a home in Sun City Center, about a mile from the care facility where JoAnn was located. Living much closer to the assisted living facility allowed me to visit more frequently. Each day, I saw that Alzheimer's was taking a greater toll on JoAnn. She could not feed herself, could not walk, and could not talk. It was almost 8 years since JoAnn was the woman I married. She no longer knew me or any of our children.

In July 2008, a new member of the facility caregiver staff named Pamela arrived. She assisted JoAnn and the other women with professional care. She had been a care-giver at a facility in South Carolina and was very professional and caring in her work. When she started feeding one of the ladies at JoAnn's table, we talked about many things and got to know each other. When I asked Pam for her phone number, her answer was, "Dick, you are married." I was extremely fortunate that my good Lord listened to my prayers and, after months of small talk at the dining room table, Pam called me on Christmas day 2008 to wish me a merry Christmas. That phone call gave me her number and we began a significant relationship. I am convinced that God had ordained Pam and me to come together as He had a specific plan for my life, and this was a part of that plan.

In 2009, Pam and I started to travel in our small Winnebago View. Before our first trip, Pam made it clear that, since I was a married man, there were several godly rules we would follow. Those rules remained in effect every day until we were married. We made our first trip to Texas to visit Peg, David, and their kids. The RV was great except when it had to cope with heavy winds. Pam was driving when the strong winds moved her and the RV a complete lane over. That was enough to convince me to purchase something more stable. When we returned to Florida, we turned in the little Winnebago View for a 42-foot Winnebago Vectra diesel. We knew the wind was not going to blow this RV off course. For the rest of 2009, we went RVing whenever we could. We truly enjoyed RVing but kept most of our travels along the East coast to include Florida, Georgia, Maryland, Virginia, West Virginia, Pennsylvania, and Tennessee. We wanted to expand our horizons but did not want to be away from home too long. In mid-2010, we ended our long-range travels because this rig got only 7-10 miles per gallon of diesel that cost $2.75 per gallon. Filling up the 100-gallon tank often cost over $200.00. We still talk about the fun RVing offered.

Once we were finished with RVing, we looked at other ways to spend our time. I was still very interested in anything to do with carpentry, so I started making some small furniture pieces and ended up purchasing a small lath. Then it was on to turning pens, wooden salt and pepper shakers, and assorted items. When we found that we had way too many pens, we decided to start a small business – "Turned for You." We bought a small display tent and off we went. The object was not to sell thousands of pens and things but, more importantly, to keep us busy. We had some fun with it, but finally lost interest and closed the business.

As the days turned into months and JoAnn's condition worsened, I was informed that she could no longer be supported in an assisted living facility and would need the care of a nursing home. Pam and I studied numerous nursing facilities and found one that appeared to be excellent. This one was located near Plant City, which was about 25 miles from the house and had a monthly cost of about $7,000. We would visit JoAnn and Pam would check that her clothes were present and clean. We would try to talk to JoAnn, but it was to no avail. She could not speak or walk or feed herself. Each morning, the staff used a lift device to carry JoAnn from the bed to the wheelchair. In the evening, they would reverse the process. All the patients spent the entire day sitting in their wheelchairs and just stared at the floor. Several years later, JoAnn passed away peacefully on January 31, 2013. She had suffered with Alzheimer's for 12 years. I pray that somehow a cure for Alzheimer's will eventually be found. You must live with someone with this miserable disease to begin to appreciate how difficult it is to see them incapable of remembering anything that took place in all the years you were together. I know our son, Tom, and his wife agree with me as they visited her in that nursing home and saw the pitiful condition she was in.

Pam and I were subsequently married and lived in the house in Sun City Center. We honestly believed that our coming together was all due to God's ordaining us for each other. Up to when I saw Pam for the first time, I never had any thought that I would care for another woman or, more importantly, take another woman as my wife. Besides being a loving wife, Pam played a critical and essential role in being there when I needed loving care. I was going through an extensive medical condition with cancer of the bladder. This led to surgery to remove the bladder and perform a urostomy. The radiation after the bladder surgery caused neuropathy in my lower right leg. It kept me from driving a vehicle. Pam had to take over all vehicle driving.

Then God helped me to start thinking about my age and how to protect Pam if something happened to me. When one pushes 80, these thoughts become more significant. I had gone through similar thoughts about JoAnn but, when I mentioned moving to a much smaller house, it did not go over well. I knew that Pam living alone in the house in Florida was not the answer because it would cost her too much each month.

The payment was close to $1,300 and the Homeowners Association was another $500. I talked to Pam about moving closer to her daughters in the Carolinas. After some discussion, we decided to take an apartment in Greenville, South Carolina. We figured we could stay there and evaluate the situation a little later. Next came selling of the house and deciding on an apartment in Greenville. We found a suitable floor plan in some new apartments and verified the availability. The house sold fast, so the movers came, and we were off to South Carolina. Pam had to do all the driving for the 600 miles and we had Tootsie Bell Bearess, the cat in the back seat, so there was no stopping overnight. We arrived at the apartment and were so grateful to have Pam's daughter and her husband, Cami and Harold, there to greet us. They had already arranged the furniture the moving van had brought. Additionally, Pam has 2 other daughters, Kristin and Meredith, as well as 3 lovely grandchildren.

Apartment living was a little different, but the problem was the 2nd story stairs. I had considerable difficulty with them so, after several months, we checked with the office and found an apartment with only 4 stairs. There still were no apartments like we wanted available on the ground floor. Then the leg problem grew worse, so the stair problem also grew. We took a 3rd apartment in two years and moved to the ground floor. I began to think about the original reason we wanted to leave Florida. It was to get Pam closer to one of her daughters. Her oldest daughter lived only 30 miles away in Central, SC. That was close enough to visit regularly but did not solve the problem of funds being available. With the apartment, it would be just as bad if I died and Pam was left with a $1,200 apartment rent. Then I began to wonder if Cami and Harold would be amenable to us moving a doublewide mobile home on their property. I had checked the price of good mobile homes and thought we could purchase one for under $100,000. When we spoke to Cami and Harold, they graciously agreed, so off we went looking at double-wide mobile homes. We found one we liked and started the arrangement for delivery. Watching the delivery was an experience! They had to move Cami's singlewide to another location on the property, and then move the 2 pieces of the doublewide into position. It was a job I would not want to undertake! Observing a doublewide mobile home on its supports is not the prettiest site to behold, so we ordered brick walls around the base of the home. We also ordered a large screened-in front porch and rear deck with a ramp for my wheelchair. Neither Pam nor I had ever lived in a mobile home, so it took a little adjusting. In a week or so, it was as nice as we could ever need. Now we had a home that was free of a mortgage.

As of this writing, Pam and I are closing in on 7 years as husband and wife. I am approaching my 86th year on Earth. I hope anyone and everyone reading this book will have as wonderful a partner as my beloved wife, Pam, and an interesting and happy life. I would like to take full credit for all that went so well but, as I wrote in the beginning, we oftentimes find that it was not us that caused many good things in our lives. I have come to appreciate that most of these changes in the direction of my life were not of my doing. They were also not a spur of the moment decision by my God. No, I believe that, long before I was born so many years ago, my heavenly Father had a plan for my life all laid out. Becoming a soldier was never my plan. I made the most unlikely soldier but, in God's grace and infinite wisdom, I became more than I could have ever dreamed. Only by His righteous right hand could this have happened to me.

Jeremiah 29:11
"For I know the plans that I have for you
declares the Lord, plans for welfare and
not calamity to give you a future and a hope."

Psalms 139: 15-16
15- "My frame was not hidden from You.
When I was made in secret, and skillfully
wrought in the depths of the earth;
16- Your eyes have seen my unformed substance;
And in Your book were all written
The days that were ordained for me,
When as yet there was not one of them."

I never appreciated this while I spent time, effort, and some sweat, working on a plan for my life. Fortunately, the 2 did not match up. Look back at your plan and your decisions and wonder if it was you or your heavenly Father that had the greatest impact on your success and your happiness. If you are certain it was you, you may want to look back again.

An Aside

I was proofreading some draft chapters of this book early on October 27, 2019 while listening to the news. They announced that JSOC forces to include Delta and Rangers in SOF Blackhawk Helicopters had raided the location of the ISIS leader, Al-Baghdadi, in Syria. During the attack, Al-Baghdadi detonated a suicide vest killing himself. Every soldier, sailor, and airman who has served with JSOC must to be so proud of these men for this significant, difficult, and dangerous mission.

AUTHOR BIO

Richard Adrian 'Dick' Scholtes was born March 18, 1934, in Joliet, Illinois. In 1950, he enlisted in the Illinois National Guard which was subsequently activated for deployment to the Korean Conflict. While training at Camp Cooke, California in preparation for movement to Korea, he was selected to attend the West Point Preparatory School and entered the academy on July 7, 1953. He was commissioned in 1957 as a second lieutenant. His first duty station was with the 82nd Airborne Division at Fort Bragg, North Carolina. He then deployed to the Panama CZ where he served as a staff officer and company commander. In 1963, Dick was selected to attend the Special Forces Officer Course at Fort Bragg, North Carolina, and the Marine Corps Amphibious Warfare Course at Quantico, Virginia. While in Vietnam from 1964 to 1965, he was the senior advisor for a Vietnamese airborne battalion and was awarded the Silver Star, two Purple Hearts, and the Bronze Star w/V. Dick. He then attended the Command and General Staff College at Fort Leavenworth, Kansas and from there he was assigned to the Infantry Branch at Fort McNair in Washington, DC. He returned to Vietnam to serve with the 1st Brigade, 5th Mechanized Division as the commander of the 1st Battalion 61st Infantry. Throughout the years, Dick was assigned to the Pentagon, 4th Mechanized Division, Brigade '76, West Point as the Brigade Tactical Officer, promoted to Brigadier

General, and reassigned to the Pentagon serving the National Military Command Center. Dick was then assigned as the Assistant Division Commander of the 82nd Airborne Division at Fort Bragg. In 1980, he was selected to establish and command a completely new organization designated as the *Joint Special Operations Command* (JSOC). He commanded this highly specialized unit four years. In 1984, Dick became the CG of the 2nd Armored Division at Fort Hood. Later, he elected to resign from the service to go before the Senate Armed Services Committee (SASC) without his General Officer Uniform. In August 1986, he went before the SASC. His presentation before the senators convinced them to direct the establishment of the United States Special Operations Command (USSOCOM) at MacDill AFB in Florida. After retirement, Dick took employment with Analytic Services, Inc. as the Vice President for Special Operations and was responsible for Mission Analysis for the newly established four-star USSOCOM. Dick retired in 2001. JoAnn died from the effects of Alzheimer's in early 2013. Dick went on to court and marry Mary Pamela Rogers and retired in South Carolina.

Made in the USA
Middletown, DE
12 August 2024